TO:

....

FROM:

....

DEVOTIONS
for the BEACH

...and days you wish you were there

BY MIRIAM DRENNAN

THOMAS NELSON
Since 1798

NASHVILLE   DALLAS   MEXICO CITY   RIO DE JANEIRO   BEIJING

Devotions for the Beach

© 2012 by Thomas Nelson, Inc.

Published in Nashville, Tennessee, by Thomas Nelson. Thomas Nelson is a registered trademark of Thomas Nelson, Inc.

Design by Studio Gearbox. Images from Thinkstock.com

Thomas Nelson®, titles may be purchased in bulk for educational, business, fund-raising, or sales promotional use. For information, please e-mail SpecialMarkets@ThomasNelson.com.

ISBN-13: 978-1-4003-2030-1

Printed in Singapore

12 13 14 15 [TWP] 5 4 3 2 1

www.thomasnelson.com

CONTENTS

BREAKFAST ON THE BEACH

Jesus said to them, "Come and eat breakfast." Yet none of the disciples dared ask Him, "Who are You?"—knowing that it was the Lord.

JOHN 24:12

It had been a tough morning, to be sure. Following Jesus' death, several disciples returned to their regularly scheduled programming. They got up early, took their fishing nets, and . . . nothing. Not a bite. Until some guy stood on the shore and called out a weird suggestion to throw their nets in from the other side of the boat.

I wonder if any of them grumbled briefly, "What difference does it make which side of the boat we throw the nets from? Who is this guy?" But by then, they were desperate enough to try anything.

Suddenly, when their nets were heavy, the same question took on a different meaning, because they knew the answer. John shouted, "It is the Lord!" and Peter could not get to Jesus fast enough. Other than suggesting that they add some of the fresh catch to His spread, Jesus' sole response was "Come and eat breakfast."

Now, wait just a minute. When read in context, the scripture notes that this is Jesus' third post-resurrection appearance, a miracle unto itself. After all, these men saw Him perish on the cross. And not only that, He's preparing a meal on the beach—not as a ghost or apparition, but as a physical being able to lift things and build a fire, etc. Then, after their own efforts had been useless, He provides an abundance of fish with one simple instruction. And after these marvels, He simply says, "Come and eat breakfast"?

Yes.

We create so much unnecessary hoopla in our own regularly scheduled programming. We plan, we implement, and we work hard . . . and get frustrated when nothing comes of it. Desperate and empty, we finally look to Jesus as a last resort—because we don't recognize who He is. And sometimes, really, all He's asking is that we come join Him and take part in what He's prepared and created. The rest will come.

So declutter your mind of plans, schedules, and "to do" lists. Instead, look out upon the waves, wiggle your toes in the sand, absorb the sights, smells, and sounds, and enjoy the moment for what it is—not what it means, not what lies ahead, not how you arrived here. There will be another time for that. For now, just be present *with Him*.

After all, in the best relationships, sometimes words are unnecessary.

Lord Jesus, I bring no words, no petitions with me right now. Just a moment to be still and commune with You in gratitude and love, using all of my senses to absorb and celebrate Your beautiful creation.

DRIFTWOOD

Some of the wise will stumble, so that they may be refined, purified and made spotless until the time of the end, for it will still come at the appointed time.

DANIEL 11:35 NIV

Usually, driftwood forms when trees or large, wooden objects have been swept away by the sea either by natural or human efforts. The pieces that make it back to shore are smooth to the touch and are often used as decorative pieces or furniture. Other pieces anchor the foundation of a sand dune, with its former life a thing of the past.

But a lot of driftwood doesn't make it back to shore. It's eaten by bacteria and organisms, and it eventually disintegrates while it drifts. A lot like what happens to us when we remain in a quandary of doubt: our stomachs churn, and we can feel as though we're being eaten from the inside out. What better way for the enemy to render us useless than to have us doubt our faith?

We may question if we were ever faithful in the first place. We might second-guess our motives or wonder if this Christian life is really worth it. Maybe God let us down and we're angry with Him—to the point that we're not speaking to Him. Or we drift because life is actually going very well—we're distracted by our new promotion, or new boyfriend, or new home, for example—so we adopt this idea that we must be doing something right, and we can therefore lighten up on living out our faith. We think that perhaps we don't need Him for everything, after all.

Then there is another reason for drifting: God's people—or those who masquerade as God's people—let you down. Sometimes, we're so fragile that all it takes is an unfriendly exchange with a greeter, neglect from a leader, or judgment from a church clique to send us packing. After all, why would we want to follow a Savior whose followers act that way? And they're the ones who represent Him?

Stay faithful. If you're hurting, stay hopeful. Pray and give thanks to God for the opportunity to grow; ask Him to shed light, ask Him for clarity. If you're experiencing a season of blessings, don't discount the Provider; invite Him to celebrate with you.

You will eventually drift, and you will eventually make it back to shore and into His loving arms. And when you do, having been purified and renewed, your knots smoothed and heart supple, you're prepared to anchor a foundation for another drifter in similar circumstances. And your former life is a thing of the past.

Lord, I have drifted away. These are lessons that I know, but lessons I have not truly learned. Search my heart and cleanse it. Show me a better way—so that I may help someone else who is struggling in the same way. Thank you for this opportunity to grow, Lord—let me not lose heart that You are in this, so I need not fear what I may be facing.

METAL DETECTORS

For where your treasure is, there your heart will be also.

LUKE 12:34

etal detecting is a curious hobby. You can see people of all ages out and about, hoping to unearth a war relic or rare jewel. Children are especially fun to watch. They shriek with delight at just about anything they find, and they guard it as a prized possession, even if it's a butter knife or toy car with only two wheels. Some folks laugh and dismiss the junk they find—they're just happy to have something interesting to do. And for others, metal detecting is serious business. They're the ones who will be out combing the beaches at the first peek of daylight, intent on finding any treasure waiting to be discovered. They often find jewelry and old coins amid a mass of junk pet tags and cigarette lighters. They see sifting through the useless as part of the hunt.

Certainly, Jesus taught about treasures in many of His parables: the lost coin, the treasure in the field. In many cases, He is asking us if our treasures align with God's purpose and values. Do we use our resources accordingly? Are we intent on searching for His treasures as we work out our own salvation? Or are we passionate about searching for our own earthly rewards without giving thought to those that are eternal?

There is a longing in our hearts that cannot be fulfilled by possessions. We laugh about "retail therapy" and taking some "me time" at the spa, but the pleasure that these bring is fleeting and temporary. Money and things are fun—they really are—but they cannot sustain our spirits. Money is a means to get through this world, but it cannot add a day to our lives. Still, we search and attempt to satisfy with things that are substandard, counterfeit—but our spirits require something much more mysterious and otherworldly.

Seeking God and His truths can be a balm to a scorched soul, bring peace to a troubled heart, and offer joy to a frazzled spirit. Let others pile up material possessions; guide your detector toward something eternal.

And when you do stumble upon one of God's many hidden treasures, shriek with delight and guard it as the prized possession it truly is.

Lord, give me a seeker's heart—one that will not be pacified with counterfeit measures and substandard trappings. Give me wisdom to discover Your truths, and I will safeguard them in my heart.

FINAL RINSE

You are already clean because of the word I have spoken to you.

JOHN 15:3 NIV

Remember as a kid running back from the beach, ravenous after a day of play? Perhaps you were headed to the car, or a beach house, or even a room at a resort, but you were racing to fill your tummy . . . and your mother would call out to you, "Stop at the spigot!" every single time. Ugh, you knew what that meant.

Outdoor showers and spigots are commonplace at the beach, yet no matter how hard we try, we can never get truly clean with them. Sure, we can get a lot of sand off of our children and ourselves, but no matter how hard we try—or how long—we still wind up tracking in sand.

Thankfully, Jesus doesn't require the same degree of cleanliness our mothers did.

Whenever we meet with the Lord, whether we realize it or not, we are ravenous. Yet He does not require us to wash off the sin we inevitably track in before we partake of time with Him. And even if He did, no matter how hard or how long we tried, we would still be wearing our sin as we approached Him. As Jesus washes us clean with His grace and forgiveness, He fills our spirits with His. For that moment, we are clean and satisfied; but we will need to cleansed another time. And another time. And another. He receives us every time, reminding us that He has taken care of it.

Lord Jesus, thank You that I may come to You wearing my sin, my guilt, my shame, and You will wash me clean.

All Together Now

As iron sharpens iron,
so a friend sharpens a friend.
PROVERBS 27:17 NLT

A study published in the journal *Proceedings of the Royal Society B* reported on a mysterious fact about Australian turtles: their eggs are buried at different depths. As a result, they receive different sun exposure causing the embryos to develop at a different pace, yet somehow all of them hatch simultaneously.

Test after test concluded that the development of the little turtles speeds up to match those turtles that are more developed in order to—putting it in overly simplified terms—meet a hatching deadline.

The scientists are still scratching their heads about this, speculating that vibrations, an exchange of a gas like carbon dioxide, or even turtles listening to one another's heartbeats can explain the phenomenon. While believers may find this fascinating, we don't attribute it to happenstance or accident. We know who orchestrated this marvel!

The God who ordained that the turtles hatch at the same time intends that we, His children, do not walk this life alone. At the most basic and most important level, the Holy Spirit is with us. At His prompting, we are also drawn to believers who are further along in their spiritual growth, even if that relationship lasts only for a season. Along the way, we ourselves will encounter others whom we can encourage along the same developmental path we've already walked, so that we may all, finally, reach the same destination; that of being more like Christ.

And just like all the little turtles hatching at the same time, these relationships are not happenstance nor accidental. When it comes to spiritual growth, whom do you look to . . . and whom are you bringing along?

Lord, thank You for sending _____, *who saw something in me that I didn't see in myself and who helped me when I didn't know I needed it. Now, as I look at* _____, *help me to understand both my purpose in her life and her purpose in mine. Please give me words and actions that honestly represent You.*

SEA OATS

"Come to me, all of you who are weary and carry heavy burdens, and I will give you rest. Take my yoke upon you. Let me teach you, because I am humble and gentle at heart, and you will find rest for your souls. For my yoke is easy to bear, and the burden I give you is light."

MATTHEW 11:28–30 NLT

Uniola paniculata—sounds like a defense weapon, doesn't it? And it is. But you know it better as the quiet, graceful, mild-mannered sea oats.

Sea oats colonies dot the landscapes of the East, Gulf, Mexican, and Caribbean coastlines, and picking them is against the law in many areas. Why is this low-maintenance grass so important?

Deep beneath the surface, the root system of these graceful, willowy grasses is strong and complex—the kind of strength the sand and soil need to hold it in place during a hurricane, tropical storm, and other extreme weather conditions. This grass catches sand and forms dunes; by all accounts, is immune to pests; and, once established, is very low maintenance. It can withstand drought, and blowing sand actually stimulates its growth. In addition, it's been suggested that, in Florida, the pygmy burrowing owl hides its nest in the sea oats colonies to offer additional protection for its young.

And for us, as we walk to the shore, the sea oats also remind us that we're almost there.

When Jesus takes hold of our hearts, there is a similar effect. We have this gentle Friend, yes, but there is so much more. He builds a root system that can withstand storms and extreme weather conditions—many of these situations actually stimulate our spiritual growth. Jesus protects and builds us, He is immune to evil, and His "yoke is easy" and His "burden is light."

And as we journey on, He gently reminds us that we're almost there.

Lord, as I look at the sea oats, I am reminded of how perfectly You crafted this world. How perfectly placed each one is, how lovely they look in the breeze, and how protective of their environment they are. I do not overlook the power and the graceful beauty that have been granted them; let them serve as a reminder to me that I not to overlook the same in You.

LETTING GO

For I will forgive their wickedness and will remember their sins no more.

HEBREWS 8:12 NIV

There's that moment. You know the moment: you're flat on your back, eyes closed, the warm sand conforming to your body . . . and you feel it, *the release.* It may take a few minutes, it may take a few days, but it will eventually come.

When it happens, you're not aware of anything or anyone else around you. The collective sighs of waves and breeze invite you to synchronize, and you accept. Eventually, you open your eyes, and their unfocused gaze absorbs the expanse that blankets your being—the sky, the horizon, the vastness of it all—without any interference.

We can liken this same open expanse to the true freedom we have by way of confessed sin—and how much greater is God's love for us. Taking our sins as far away as possible, He forgives, forgets, and washes us clean. We don't have this ability, but we can reap its eternal benefits.

So when that moment occurs, when all is released and you're enveloped by the vast sky and infinite horizon, capture it in your mind and embed it in your heart. Think about how many miles your eyes and thoughts can travel, and meditate on the fact that God's forgiveness reaches even farther, beyond anything we can imagine, and that His love is just as boundless. "As far as the east is from the west, so far has He removed our transgressions from us" (Psalm 103:12).

Soon enough, you will return to chaotic mornings, pediatrician appointments, work stresses, nonstop interruptions, and you'll be at the brink of imploding—but wait. Whether you're waiting in line at the grocer or sitting in the parking lot at your child's school, take a few moments to recall. Go back to lying on that sand and letting go. Remember just how far He can remove your sin and just how vast, how unfettered, is His love.

Just like that first time on the beach, getting there may take longer at first, but eventually the release comes quicker. Release your sin; relinquish your burdensome guilt. And receive, without interference, His boundless love.

Father, thank You for allowing me the opportunity to confess sin after conviction and in prayer. And thank You that Your forgiveness is boundless. Lord, I have experienced only a portion of the breadth and depth of Your forgiveness, but enough to know that it frees my soul from death and nurtures my spirit during those times I have difficulty forgiving myself.

SWIMSUIT COVER-UPS:
THE GOOD, THE BAD, AND THE UGLY

But Shem and Japheth took a garment, laid it on both their shoulders,
and went backward and covered the nakedness of their father.

GENESIS 9:23

S kimpy, full-bodied, sarongs, zip-ups, pullovers, hooded, frilly, strapless—
swimsuit cover-ups serve one purpose: to cover our nakedness so that we can
jiggle from Point A to Point B without everyone seeing every dimple, scar, and extra
pound. They do not take away the flaws. They just hide them from full-on exposure.

The flood was over. Noah was now a farmer and had planted a vineyard. He
became drunk, disrobed, and eventually passed out, fully exposed. His youngest
son, Ham, saw this and, instead of helping Noah, elected to tell his brothers about
it instead. Was he laughing? Was he being melodramatic? Was he telling them as
a "prayer request?" Who knows—but we do know that Ham's intentions weren't
honorable. When Noah awoke, he remembered enough of what had happened and
cursed him while blessing his other two sons, who had taken the time to cover up
their father and say nothing more of the incident.

In a sense, Shem and Japheth covered their father with their own dignity to
spare him further exposure and humiliation. Why, oh why, do we not do the same?

Let's face it, sisters . . . we are not always kind to each other. Not in the work-
place. Not on the basketball sidelines. Not at the school fundraisers or neighborhood cookouts. So it's irrelevant if we even try to be at church. We can be petty and
biting. And that's just with the ones we know and love!

We do this because we've all at some point been the one who isn't known and therefore isn't loved—and we fear we'll be in exile again. We never want to be the odd woman out, and, ironically enough, we often succeed at the exclusion of someone else.

Acceptance and approval have such a strong hold on us, no matter who or what group is doing the holding. In order to gain a bit more power in the hierarchy of the group or not be cast away, we'll disregard whether or not what's being said about another woman is true; break her confidence; tear her down because we are either jealous of or repulsed by her appearance; and cover up our own weaknesses and issues rather than cover her with God's love.

Swimsuit cover-ups come in all varieties, chosen on personal style and, yes, function. We can love the unloved the same way. Challenge yourself to be someone who clothes others with dignity and respect, particularly someone whose flaws have been on display too long. That person has suffered enough.

Lord, help me shrug off whatever issues I've had with those who are publicly cast aside. Their sin is not for me to judge. You made them and highly prize them. Help me to be mindful of this and approach them with the same love You have poured into me.

MESSAGES

[The teachers of the law and the Pharisees] were using this question as a trap,
in order to have a basis for accusing [Jesus].
But Jesus bent down and started to write on the ground with his finger.
When they kept on questioning him, he straightened up and said to them,
"If any one of you is without sin, let him be the first to throw a stone at her."
Again he stooped down and wrote on the ground.

JOHN 8:6–8 NIV

What was Jesus writing?

It's fun to write messages in the sand; it can also be cathartic. Some people take photos of their messages to send to friends; others may stand and watch as the waves take the message away, as though it never existed.

What was Jesus writing?

A woman had been caught in adultery, and she was brought to Jesus. There was a group assembled, so the Pharisees "reminded" Jesus that, according to Moses' law, she should be stoned, but they wanted to know what He had to say. Not once, but twice, Jesus stooped and wrote on the ground with His finger, and there is mysterious significance as to why John included this detail in the passage. Now, we shouldn't miss what Jesus said in between His stooping—which is fairly critical to the story—but what was He writing?

Some believe that He was writing the Pharisees names and possibly their sins. This theory is based primarily on Jeremiah 17:13: "Those who depart from Me shall be written in the earth, because they have forsaken the LORD, the fountain of living waters." In the preceding chapter from John, Jesus spoke of Himself as living water. So perhaps He was fulfilling a prophecy. Others believe it was to demonstrate, as God the Father did when He carved the Ten Commandments with His finger, that Jesus had the authority to issue two new commandments: for us to love one another, as He loved us (John 13:34), and to bear one another's burdens, as indicated by Paul in Galatians 6:2.

We don't know for sure what Jesus was writing, nor do we know who saw His message. It's possible, however, that once the crowd had dispersed and He was left to deal with the woman Himself, He'd written only one other word: forgiven.

And whether that message was erased by Him or the wind, her sins were forgiven.

Lord Jesus, by Your blood and resurrection, You provided a way for my sins to be erased. Though others may try to condemn me, You do not. I need only come to You for this gift. There is nothing more I can do for salvation.

Raining at the Beach

Better is a neighbor nearby than a brother far away.

PROVERBS 27:10

It's not unusual for an afternoon pop-up shower to occur on the beach, but it is an inconvenience. This isn't supposed to happen on your vacation—you're on borrowed time with the ocean, after all! Can't this wait until you've pulled out of the parking lot for the last time? And now you have to be cooped up with your kids or friends until this shower blows over. So irritating. So inconvenient.

We often treat our friends with the same regard: *Oh, not again! Can't they wait? This is just not a good time.*

Let's be honest here. When's the last time you allowed yourself to be inconvenienced by a friend? If she called now, would you give your undivided attention, or would you allow your children to constantly interrupt while she is speaking from the heart? If she left a tearful message, would you call her back immediately—or wait until it was convenient for you? Would you offer to come and merely sit with her? Would you reassure her that you are there for her?

Maybe the issue she's dealing with seems fairly open and shut; maybe she's involved in something you disapprove of; maybe her life seems so simple and easy compared to yours. But there really is no excuse for not being there for her—not if she's your friend. And not if you are hers.

"But you don't understand!" you protest. "I have young kids, I'm trying to work part-time, and there's just never a good time to call with all of my responsibilities. And the stuff she's dealing with? It's always the same. Some guy dumped her, or she hates her job. I mean, my problems are real. My life is real. This is just same-old, same-old with her. I can't identify with it, and I can't fix it for her."

You're right: you can't fix it for her. Nor is she asking for priority over your "real" life—just a bit of your time. Rest assured that you have inconvenienced her at some point too. Now it's your turn to be inconvenienced.

Someday, you will need her again, and, just like a summer shower, we don't always get to pick those days. Neither do your friends—not real friends, anyway. You see, Proverbs 17:17 instructs us to love our friends at all times—not just the convenient ones.

Lord, I have taken my friendship with Your daughter _____ for granted. When I reach out to her, I will ask for forgiveness. I will set aside time to extend to her the love that You have given me. Give me ears that listen the way You would have me listen. And if I do speak, Father, please provide the words so that I may speak the truth in love.

FLIP-FLOPS

"If any place will not welcome you or listen to you, leave that place and
shake the dust off your feet as a testimony against them."

MARK 6:11 NIV 2011

lip. Flop. Flip. Flop. Flip. Flop. Listen to the sound your flip-flops make: your foot grips to them as sand swooshes in and out between your heel and the sole. Sometimes the sand feels nice as it glides through, but eventually, it annoys and aggravates—kind of like when we are rejected after having shared the gospel.

Today's scripture refers to an ancient Jewish practice of shaking the dust off their feet after passing through a Gentile-populated area to indicate that Gentiles did not influence them. For Jesus to suggest that this practice be upheld for Jews who reject the Good News, then, sent a clear message that His followers would remain separate from them too.

There are two things we need to be mindful of when we share Christ with someone and she does not accept Him; first, her rejection is not of us, but of God (1 Thessalonians 4:8); and secondly, it's possible that she may return to Him later (Philemon 15-16). We cannot "save" anyone; nor are we guaranteed that any part of our message will be received—all we are called to do is deliver it. Arguing or retaliating isn't necessary—their ears, hearts, and minds are closed, and this kind of reaction does not represent our Jesus.

But what if the one who rejects Him is a close friend or family member? We can't exactly walk away, and we may endure a bit of hostility further on. Love them, anyway. Stay above the ridicule, work to avoid any conflicts. They don't understand why you're "that way," and resentment will assuredly come—after all, shouldn't you be angry with them? Joy and *agape* love may be foreign concepts to them—but as a believer, they aren't to you. And we know that love covers a multitude of sins (1 Peter 4:8). So love them anyway.

You have done your part—now let God do His. He doesn't owe us any further explanation. Shake it off.

Abba, Father, give me the words and actions that testify to Your salvation. And when I share, prepare me for rejection, yet keep me hopeful for reconciliation—let me not be discouraged. Thank You for freeing me from the burden of saving anyone—I can deliver Your message, knowing that its receipt is up to You and up to them.

SANDSPURS

And lest I should be exalted above measure by the abundance of the revelations,

a thorn in the flesh was given to me, a messenger of Satan to buffet me,

lest I be exalted above measure.

2 CORINTHIANS 12:7

Once you've stepped on one, you never forget. And they have ways to ensure that. Sandspurs are grassy plants with prickly blooms. They are unforgiving if they take hold of your skin, and if the spines break off underneath the skin's surface, then you've borrowed even more trouble.

Some coastal natives will tell you that even as the soles of their feet become tougher during barefoot seasons, the sandspur's pods and spines become even more brittle and therefore pricklier. If you attempt to cut sandspurs, you'll actually spread its seeds even more. And if your bare feet manage to withstand them, they'll find ways to pierce other parts of your flesh.

The coastal sandspur is known as *Cenchrus incertus*, which, loosely translated, means "uncertain seeds." This is also an accurate description for the thorns in our own flesh.

Much speculation has been given to Paul's "thorn." He himself did not specify what it was, and more than likely there was more than one. We know from Paul's past that he was highly regarded, very well educated, a tentmaker by trade, and a proud, respected member of the Sanhedrin. Once he turned his life over to Christ, he pursued his work with even greater zeal, tirelessly reaching out to anyone willing to hear the good news—and even to a few who weren't. So even though his leadership and responsibilities were growing, and he was gaining the respect of a different crowd, that didn't mean pride was no longer an issue. Paul had to find a way to manage it.

We see this happen in different kinds of leadership roles today—church committees, celebrities, elected officials, pastors, managers—no one is immune. Including you and me.

In the rest of this passage, we learn that Paul dislikes his predicament, but has concluded that, though painful, it is somehow in his best interest that the thorn remain. For one thing, it serves as a constant reminder that God is in control; secondly, it requires his petition for a strength that he cannot attain on his own (v. 9).

This is how Paul chose to handle the uncertain seeds that remained rooted in him. How are you handling yours?

Father God, I've been guilty of complaining about my thorns instead of seeing them as reminders from You. Starting today, I acknowledge that You are in control and that Your strength and grace are indeed sufficient for me, no matter how difficult a person or situation may get. Give me wisdom for remaining rooted in You so that my words and actions consistently reflect Your love.

BOAT SHOES

But may the God of all grace, who called us to His eternal glory by Christ Jesus,
after you have suffered a while, perfect, establish, strengthen, and settle you.

1 PETER 5:10

There are just some things that work better once they're broken in, and boat shoes are a prime example. Canvas or leather, their nonmarking rubber soles have a pattern cut into the bottom that gives the wearer extra grip on a wet deck. When the leather ones are rubbed with oil, they repel water. Sailing enthusiasts will tell you, when these shoes are salt-logged and floppy, they simply work better and are far more comfortable.

Believers, we need to take a cue.

How exciting it is when we are reborn! In the newness of it all, we explode with joy and happiness at what's been done for us! We're going to save the world just as we've been saved! We're gonna right some wrongs! We're gonna get our friends in line! But we're squeaky, we rub people the wrong way, and we're tied too tight. Just like new boat shoes.

Oh, we've got the right idea about helping others find Jesus—letting others know the Source of our joy, and carrying out our faith in works. But we're not broken in; we're not as effective. Yet.

Hardships will eventually come. Complacency. Bad decisions. Hurts. The salt that penetrates our wounds. There are also other factors. Mentors who gently guide us. Life events. Distractions. Celebrations. Personal relationships that make us think. People who challenge us. All of these valuable contributions break us in and make us salt-logged and floppy.

If you're newly acquainted with Jesus, take care not to wear people out, particularly other believers; and remember that the newness will wear off. We're just praying that your joy doesn't fade with it. If you're a few steps farther along in your walk, take it easy on the new believer: be a source of encouragement, stay calm, and be gentle. Remember, you can only lead as far as you've traveled.

Father God, I am reminded of Your grace and mercy. My heart explodes with joy when I think about these things! Help me recognize and help others who do not know You, but give me wisdom to approach these relationships with love and authenticity, with words that reflect who You are.

GRAIN OF TRUTH

I knew you before I formed you in your mother's womb.
Before you were born I set you apart
and appointed you as my spokesman to the world.

JEREMIAH 4:5 NLT

ave you ever seen photographs of individual grains of sand blown up over 250 times their actual size? Some grains look like red, glossy stones, others look like icicles; some resemble speckled yellow and brown eggs, and still others seem shaped like corncobs, snowflakes, and precious gems. Some grains are square; some, spherical; and some, flat. No two grains are the same—in fact, you'd never know you were even looking at grains of sand if no one told you.

So the next time your toes are gripping the warm sand, think about each and every tiny grain, unique in shape, depth, color, and texture. God created each and every one of this infinite variety of grains.

Since God shows off His creative abilities in tiny bits of sand, think about what He has done—and can do—with us, the crown of His creation. Each one of us is unique in appearance, personality, gifts, and experiences; each of us is wired with feelings, preferences, responses and tastes that are ours alone.

Too often, however, we try to model ourselves after another person. We want to dress like her, speak as she does, wear our hair the same way, or, worse yet, allow her opinions to become our own—and the list can go on. Whether the object of our admiration is a friend, celebrity, or church leader—yes, even a beloved Bible study teacher or ministry leader—we lose ourselves in trying to be like her. Our reasons for doing so vary, but the key issue is dissatisfaction with ourselves.

As believers, however, we have within us the Holy Spirit who is using His power to, among other things, transform us into the Christlike image God created us to have. No one else possesses this ability to transform us, regardless of how spiritual, beautiful, or "together" someone appears.

The Lord knows why each grain of sand is a certain way, and He knows the same about you. Lean into Him to find out why you have the characteristics you have and what purposes He has in mind for you.

Lord, thank You for wiring me the way You have, and I ask You to reveal to me how You will use me in Your kingdom work. Thank You for giving me the free will to accept or reject Your intended purposes. Today, right now, I pray that I will choose to accept them.

SEAGULLS

On the right they will devour,
but still be hungry;
on the left they will eat,
but not be satisfied.

ISAIAH 9:20 NIV

There they are—those squeaky little sirens that either annoy or delight you, depending on where they are and how long they linger.

Seagulls are as integral to the beach as rocks, sand, and waves. If you think about it, a beach without seagulls is a scary, lonely place, indicative of treacherous weather. Their presence helps identify where you are and reinforce that conditions are, at the very least, bearable.

But what happens when you feed them? Well, it's fun for a while, giving a crumb or two to those that dare approach . . . until you're surrounded by all their friends. And their numbers grow larger, their demands grow louder, and you're swatting them away, wishing you'd never entertained them in the first place. You run—but they follow.

Insecurities are like seagulls. In a way, they identify where you are in your spiritual journey, and they reinforce your humanity. From a distance, you consider entertaining one or two—that new purse you really can't afford or the juicy tidbit of gossip that would put you in with the right crowd if shared. There's no harm, after all, in wanting to look good or have friends, right?

But what happens when you feed your insecurities?

Lord, thank You for my weaknesses and faults. They help me identify my sin and transgressions. Give me strength not to feed them. Let me, instead, ask You to feed my soul because that is the only way my insecurities will be silenced . . . and one day, either here or in heaven, exist no more.

BUOYS

And I said: "O my God, I am too ashamed and
humiliated to lift up my face to You, my God;
for our iniquities have risen higher than our heads,
and our guilt has grown up to the heavens."

EZRA 9:6

They hold up docks, secure nets, save people. Buoys of all kinds serve one purpose: to lift up and support. They are always there, quietly bobbing along. We tend to overlook them except in times of need, such as inclement weather or life-threatening situations.

Ezra was fully aware that he and the rest of the Israelites were drowning in sin. Granted, Ezra had not sinned in the same manner as others—but he recognized that he, too, was a sinner and not perfect. He was, perhaps, far more sensitive to sin than most.

Do you find this to be true in your own spiritual walk? You see sin all around you and within you, and yet the more you grow in faith, the more sensitive you become to it? Look again at Ezra's prayer. How often do we feel our sin or situation is so hopeless, so awful, that we feel it's beyond even asking for forgiveness? Whether it's an individual or collective sin, we are resigned to the attitude that it cannot change—and, thus, we cannot be changed.

Without buoys, docks float away, nets sink to the ocean floor, and lives are lost. Without God, we suffer the same fate.

So, interestingly enough, we have a choice: embrace and confess our sin or turn away from God in guilt. As we become more sensitive to sin, we realize this is the Holy Spirit working in us. So while we may not sin the same way as the next person does, we are recognizing that there is no hierarchy to sin. We are catching a glimpse of the way God sees it. Grab hold of this type of experience instead of drowning in shame, for conviction of sin does refine character.

If, however, we choose to succumb to our guilt, then we are suggesting that our sin or situation is beyond God's power. We doubt this is something He can handle, and our hearts are hardened toward Him.

We need a buoy to secure us—and, in tandem, perhaps secure others.

You see, secure docks can then secure boats, and secure nets catch fish—they cannot function properly without buoys. No matter how deeply the nets sink, the buoys hold them until it's time for them to be lifted.

God holds us in the same way, to use us in the same manner for His kingdom.

Father, thanks to the sacrifice of Your Son, I am able to lift my face and confess. I praise You that my heart and mind are increasingly sensitive to my own sin and to that which is around me. Lord, I pray I will come to You in haste each time I recognize my sin, instead of drowning in my guilt and shame.

DOLPHINS

Then your light shall break forth like the morning,
Your healing shall spring forth speedily,
And your righteousness shall go before you;
The glory of the LORD shall be your rear guard.

ISAIAH 58:8

O h, they are so playful, leaping, jumping, talking to one another. They tease us, swimming along with their fins just above the ocean's surface. We do a double take, just to make sure it is, in fact, a teasing dolphin instead of a hungry shark. Play is as important to dolphins as they are to one another.

Dolphins are very social creatures and as such, establish strong bonds. They take care of one another, making sure any who are infirmed stay fed and are taken to the surface to breathe. In fact, dolphins will extend this care and protection to other species, including whales and humans. When one of the pod is lost, they grieve.

Another remarkable fact—albeit a mysterious one—is their ability to heal quickly from injury, even something as deep and extensive as a shark bite. Infection is very rare and, miraculously, their bodies heal in a way that restores their original contours. We know this is God's creative design—and there are, of course, lessons we can take from it.

Today's passage concerns our personal acts of worship and our service. Specifically, they are to be sincere. For example, if we fast, we should be certain of our reasons and not make a public display of our sacrifice. And our works should stem from our sincere love for and worship of the Lord—who may choose to bring about a speedy healing for others or possibly ourselves.

Very often, God isn't one-sided in His blessings. Think about it: how many times have we taken a mission trip or worked a volunteer event and come back feeling almost selfish, as though maybe we got more out of our service than we put in? The mission met a specific need, and the unexpected joy you received met another. When we respond to God's call, we are the recipients of this joy.

Dolphins connect with others, communicate with others, and help others—even at their own risk. They get caught up in nets, they storm sharks, and they are unwilling to leave a weaker creature behind. Sometimes, given their playful nature, we forget their bravery. So while we may not understand how the dolphin heals so quickly and cleanly, we do know *why* . . . and *who's* behind it.

What kind of healing do you need? When we reach out with a sincere, worshipful heart and help meet the needs of others, we often receive the blessing of healing for ourselves.

Lord, what a magnificent creature You made in the dolphin! They're intelligent, they're fun, they're protective, they're caretakers. How can I be more like them? Show me.

KNOWING TOO MUCH

It is the glory of God to conceal a matter;
to search out a matter is the glory of kings.

PROVERBS 25:2 NIV

Every girls' beach trip has a planner in the group; otherwise, there would be no girls' beach trip. To make arrangements and get things organized is one thing; but sometimes, there'll be one in the group who researches your rental, scopes out area restaurants, checks the weather/beach reports down to the hour, downloads a few coupons to various attractions, and knows exactly how each day should be spent. There. Done. Nothing left to chance. Just thinking about doing all that work can make you feel exhausted and you haven't even left the driveway. Why?

There is such a thing as knowing too much. Look no further than the Fall as an example.

God instructed Adam not to touch the Tree of the Knowledge of Good and Evil because he would die. That's all Adam needed to know. Since God was trustworthy, the *why* wasn't necessary. But we know what happened next. And what's been happening ever since.

After all, how many of us meet a guy and the first thing we do is "google" him? Or we want the play-by-play on our neighbors' divorce—but for what purpose? Or if we learn a supposed friend has been bad-mouthing us, what do we gain by knowing every last syllable that was said?

Whether we're reading too much into a relationship, seeking our own validation, or building our case, we are past the point of making informed decisions. We're looking for total control, nothing left to chance. We're nobody's fool, after all.

Having the facts—the real facts—is important. And again, God gave us noggins to make informed decisions. But assumptions we create in our own minds and statements that use the word *probably* or begin with *I heard* do not fall under the category of facts. They may be true . . . but they may not be. Even our Internet searches cannot reveal either the full story or a person's heart.

So you may know it all—or, at the very least, which stones are left to turn—but what do you gain from it? Ironically enough, more pain. Or a squashed opportunity. Or new ideas that will color the situation as you move forward.

Can you let go of the incessant need to know everything and trust that God's timing—and His concealing—are in your best interest? Challenge yourself to let go of something you've been trying to get details on—particularly if it's a situation where you already know the truth. Think about where it all started, in that garden so long ago. You already know how the story ends. He wins. And as His children, so do we.

Lord, I ask for Your help as I let go of all the little details surrounding _____. I know the general truth, and someday, I may know the rest. But for now, my "rest" lies within what You know and choose to conceal. I trust You, Lord, that it is best for me not to know.

CALMING OR CRASHING?

Then He arose and rebuked the wind, and said to the sea,
"Peace, be still!" And the wind ceased and there was a great calm.

MARK 4:39

O nce the sound captures you, it lulls you into an almost trancelike state. Minutes, even hours can pass before you know it. To get there, you must be silent.
To stay there, you must be still. And the waves will draw you into deeper silence,
deeper stillness, deeper, deeper still.

There's little dispute that watching and listening to the ocean—the rhythm
and repetition, the graceful waves—reduces stress and calms nerves. Any number
of CDs and DVDs offer nice replications of the experience, but nothing compares
to the original, live show.

In an instant, however, this same environment can make us anxious and fearful.

It's ironic that the words normally associated with the calming, comforting effect are not calming words—the *crashing* waves, the *roaring* surf. If you think about
it, these exact phrases can also be used to describe stormy conditions.

So, who's in charge of the context? And who should be?

Let me preface today's passage: All day Jesus sat in a boat, teaching. The boat was
in a lake, so there were no rolling waves along the shoreline. The water was obviously
calm. Later that night, however, Jesus and His disciples were traveling to the other
side, and a massive storm erupted. Waves and wind tossed the little boat around. (Can
you imagine the nausea as they feverishly bailed water?). How can a situation that is
so calm one minute be so hazardous the next? And all Jesus could do was sleep?! Seri-
ously?! The disciples needed all hands on deck!

Panicked, they ran to Jesus and woke Him up. He rose and simply told the storm to stop. (Did He sigh an exasperated sigh first?) He didn't have to ask what was wrong, which reinforces the point He made to His disciples that night: *He was aware, even though it didn't appear that way to them.*

They didn't need all hands on deck; they just needed Jesus. They needed to trust that He was there.

When you look across the ocean and feel that calming lull, consider also the storms that have visited that exact spot. Similarly, is there someone or something in your life who has brought you both joy and sorrow? Where peace and calamity somehow coexisted? Who is in charge of the context?

As your frazzled nerves and tightened muscles give way to the sight and sound of peaceful waves, and you're thinking about this situation or person, take to heart the command of our Lord: "Peace, be still!" Let Him draw you in, into deeper silence, deeper stillness, deeper, deeper still.

Lord, I sit. I stare. I hear. But I'm not there. There is a squall in my spirit that You know about and that You are handling. Wash over me as the waves do the sand. I need not fear—You are in the context.

FULGURITES

*Now the Spirit expressly says that in latter times some will depart from the faith,
giving heed to deceiving spirits and doctrines of demons, speaking lies in hypocrisy,
having their own conscience seared with a hot iron, forbidding to marry,
and commanding to abstain from foods which God created to be received
with thanksgiving by those who believe and know the truth. . . .
For bodily exercise profits a little, but godliness is profitable for all things,
having promise of the life that now is and of that which is to come.*

1 TIMOTHY 4:1–3, 8

When lightning strikes sand, it melts into a tubular structure known as a *fulgurite*. Its shape follows the path of the bolt as it travels through the sand, instantly melting the sand in its path, sealing it by accumulating an outer layer of sand that adheres to itself, but does not melt or melt fully. While the matter is still a form of quartz, it's no longer sand; it becomes something entirely different from its original form.

Paul's advice to Timothy concerned well-intended believers who were deceived in the same way. Instead of abiding in Jesus, their minds are "seared with a hot iron" by false teachings. In an attempt to be spiritually disciplined, they miss the point of grace.

For at least two thousand years, movements, trends, and fads have passed through Christendom, remaking everything in its course into something entirely different—and making some people obsessed with the new trend. Look at the various diet programs, financial seminars, dating trends, music, and worship practices

50

that claim to have a Christian basis. Many bear no resemblance to our Savior, and they usually lead to much discord among the body of believers.

We need to stop following everyone and everything that slaps on a *Christian* label. We need, instead, to truly examine things through the lens of Scripture. It is a safe assumption that the enemy will find subtle and clever ways to distort truth, particularly by way of legalism and prejudice. Assess these trends with a discerning nature, instead of taking someone else's word for it. If someone or something is claiming to be Christian, we should be on alert, for that is quite a claim.

All of God's creation is good. And no one is suggesting that we indulge in gluttony or we need not exercise—but Paul was very clear that obsessions with these things, even as a sincere act of worship, only "profits a little." There are just some dos and don'ts for which we need to trust the Holy Spirit's counsel.

If you stumble upon a fulgurite, pick it up. They're usually just a few inches below the surface. Be reminded that Christ has already made us into a new creation. No trend, television program, seminar, diet, CD, book, or person truly possesses the same power.

Lord, there is no substitute for You. As I study Your Word and spend time in prayer, please let me choose any supplemental resources or acts of worship with great care to ensure that I am not led astray nor lead others astray. Keep my heart pure and sincere.

FOOTPRINTS

You enlarged my path under me;
So my feet did not slip.

2 SAMUEL 22:37

Go out on the beach early in the morning, and you'll likely find a set of tracks in the sand. They can be paw prints from a dog, claw prints from a bird, human footprints, or even some that are unidentifiable. The next time you see tracks, let your eyes follow them for just a bit. Look ahead to observe the direction. Do they continue on straight, or do they meander? Are the impressions faint or bold? Farther down, do the prints vanish?

A lot of times, we will follow others' whims and fancies. Over time, they meander and fade—and since we're following someone else's steps, they do not truly represent our own paths.

Now see if you can locate some footprints large enough that your own feet fit inside. Try to follow them; place your own feet inside the imprints. Any chance your stride is larger? Maybe you find yourself, at times, jumping from one footprint to the next. You're wondering if, in fact, you're stepping in the footsteps of Paul Bunyan himself!

As you stop to catch your breath, reflect on God's law. We certainly want to follow God's law, but admittedly, it is exhausting. Who can keep up? Who can land in each and every step correctly? Although it guides our steps—and again, it should—it also helps us recognize that we need a Savior. We need One who will carry us from one step to the next. One whose own steps are so large, they completely cover the original steps we tried to follow (Psalm 17:5).

In effect, the original steps are still there, but Jesus' steps have eliminated the chasms in between.

Lord, as I try to follow Your precepts, I recognize my need for a smoother path and a way that forgives my stumbling attempts. Thank You for giving me a sure path to You in Your Son, Jesus.

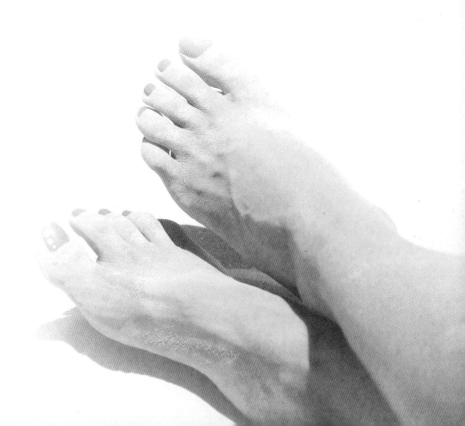

Good-Byes

"And surely I am with you always, to the very end of the age."

Matthew 28:20 NIV

D o we have to leave?"

"Can't we stay just a little longer?"

Perhaps the saddest part about visiting a beach is leaving it. You pack up, you say your good-byes to friends, and you imagine that the beach may even be a bit sad about your departure as well.

Some of us depart in a flurry of activity. We busy ourselves with packing, sweeping, thinking that the quicker our departure, the fewer our heart pangs and the easier it will be to resume our routines. Others of us linger, leaving hours after our scheduled departure times, wanting one last look, one last hug, one last memory.

How often do these kinds of good-byes happen in your prayer life?

There are days we race through, as though God is an item to check off our "to do" lists. The sooner we can get through it, the sooner we can get on with the day.

Then there are times when those clamoring voices vying for attention will just have to wait; you want to spend time with your Maker. You've reached your end, and you want nothing more than to be still in Him. So you linger, remaining there as long as possible because of the peace, the comfort, and the rest you feel.

When's the last time you had that sort of communion with the Lord, when you wanted to remain in His glorious presence because there was something about that particular moment that drew you in, drew you closer?

When you experience those moments, drink deeply. Receive Jesus, welcome Him, linger with Him. As in any good conversation, give Him time to speak and yourself time to listen. If your soul feels parched, ask Him to quench it in this way.

When the day becomes busy, as it surely will, stay mindful that He remains with you. He is there and present.

This was Jesus' promise to the disciples and to us as He returned to the Father. We may not completely understand how He does this, but we can be certain that this is no hurdle for the One who conquered death. With Him, there are no good-byes.

Lord, thank You for abiding with me even when my commitment to abide with You wanes or I am distracted.

WHAT LIES BENEATH . . . AND AMONG

These were [Jesus'] instructions to [His disciples]:
"The harvest is great, but the workers are few.
So pray to the Lord who is in charge of the harvest;
ask him to send more workers into his fields."

LUKE 10:2 NLT

The next time you're standing knee-deep in the ocean, try to wrap your mind around the fact that scientists estimate up to 80 percent of all life on our planet is found beneath the ocean's surface, that 99 percent of all living space is contained within our oceans, and that humans have explored less than 10 percent of it.

These statistics should humble us who sometimes pride ourselves in our far-reaching efforts to reach the world for Christ. We pity those people whose worldview does not stretch past their own community, because *we* have traveled to faraway lands and therefore *know* how the world works. But considering that 89 percent of our planet's living space has yet to be explored, we don't know as much as we may think we do.

Consider the truth that we often don't grasp the kind of poverty that exists in other countries until we visit those nations. Quite frankly, however, we often miss the lost and the poor who are living within a stone's throw of our own homes. We have not yet explored our own communities for ways to serve God.

There are hungry people, homeless people, and hopeless people all around you. And although Jesus said the poor would always be among us (John 12:8), we are not to ignore them or, directly or indirectly, keep them that way. We are to work—either on a local or a global scale—to provide them with food, shelter, clothing, justice, and the good news about Jesus' death and resurrection, God's forgiveness, and the promise of eternal life. Our service may be something as simple as buying a parched-looking stranger a bottle of water or as far-reaching as building a water-treatment system for an entire village. Whenever we do these things in Jesus' name, we are in sync with His eternal purpose and in relationship with Him in a way that brings Him glory—a relationship that we can enjoy forever.

We are a small but a very significant part of God's creation. He entrusted us with His message. So, when you stand at the ocean's edge, think about all the un-explored life that lurks just beneath the surface—and ponder the unexplored lives around you who need to hear the good Lord's message of hope and love.

Lord, as You keep my head bowed in gratitude and humility, please also keep my eyes and ears open for every opportunity to shine Your light into someone elses dark life. I am ready to explore my community and even more of Your big world in order to find those You want me to serve in Your name.

WASHED-UP REMNANTS

Let us go right into the presence of God with sincere hearts fully trusting him.
For our guilty consciences have been sprinkled with Christ's blood to make us clean,
and our bodies have been washed with pure water.

HEBREWS 10:22 NLT

The most interesting things can wash up on shore—remnants of a larger story that we are not privy to; evidence of another time that has passed; items that don't belong in the ocean but are now a part of the beach scene. A child's shoe that was taken out to sea; a fishing rod that slipped out of a fishing boat; sunglasses that were jarred loose when the wearer was hit by a powerful wave—these pieces of stories remind us that the sea has the final say on their destination and configuration.

In the same way, sin didn't belong in God's original landscape, nor was it intended for the human race. Nonetheless, it is now part of our reality and, collectively, part of our story. Tossed about, our random episodes of past sin wash ashore to lie in full view, and as we stroll by to take a closer look, we are forced to decide: Will we keep walking and leave it for someone else to clean up? Or maybe stomp it into the sand to disappear . . . for a while? Or maybe we decide it's time to face our sin. It's time to pick it up and put it in the garbage once and for all.

Unless or until we do this, and ask God's help in the process, the cycle of sin's stronghold will continue to ebb and flow in our lives, keeping us from truly experiencing the fullness of grace He's waiting to lavish on us. Fortunately, we can look forward to indescribable peace in knowing that the Lord (not the sea) has the final say on our sin's destination. "He washed away our sins, giving us a new birth and new life through the Holy Spirit" (Titus 3:5 NLT).

Father, I have so many random pieces of hurt and sin that I know don't belong in my life. Help me, fill me with Your strength to put them away once and for all. Help me fully realize the fact that, while they have collectively made up my story today, they don't have to define my story tomorrow. Thank You for washing my sins away and for filling me instead with Your love and forgiveness. All praise to You!

VOLLEYBALL GAMES

I do not understand what I do.

For what I want to do I do not do, but what I hate I do.

ROMANS 7:15 NIV

S *ay what?*

Kind of makes your head spin, doesn't it? Paul could be delightfully convoluted sometimes. You can practically see his two hands, gesturing back and forth, as you read this verse and the subsequent verses. It's like watching a volleyball game of words and will.

Volleyball is a fun game, whether you're a spectator or player. It's suspenseful, particularly if the ball is kept in the air for a long period of time. It bounces from player to player, across the net, back and forth, and the stakes grow higher the longer the ball remains in play. Who will dive for it? Who will miss? When this happens, players and crowd alike will often react with each hit.

The internal struggle Paul described in Romans 7 isn't as much fun. We go back and forth with sin. We willingly participate, hating ourselves for our own weakness, questioning how real our faith is, wondering if we are really saved. We have periods when we feel like giving up and giving in, and sometimes we do. But God doesn't. He knew in the beginning, and knows now that we need a Savior.

Still, there are those times when, regardless of what we've learned and how far we've come, we *want* to bounce back over. Maybe life was more exciting then or you were having more fun, or making more money, or had more dates, or . . . or . . . Maybe if we just take a little taste of what we're missing, then we'll bounce back over to the other side of the net? Just a quick visit. After all, if Christ took care of the game point already, why should we be concerned?

Thankfully, Paul covered this in Romans 6 by asking a very important question: "What benefit did you reap at that time from the things you are now ashamed of?" (v. 21 NIV). Now, be honest with yourself and your Lord as you answer this question: How does that "benefit" compare to a peaceful mind and heart in the present? How does that choice to sin show gratitude for the eternal life in the future?

We can take heart that Paul struggled as we do, and was honest enough to write down the crazy game that plays out in our minds, hearts, and actions. But, honestly, aren't you tired of playing?

Lord, lately I've been wondering if I'd be better off going back to _____. It just seems like life was more _____ back then, but I know our relationship would suffer. I ask, first, for forgiveness and, second, for strength and patience as I want You to work on my heart and mind so that I may overcome this urge. And because I know You're You, please take this part of my past and use it toward Your glory.

VESSELS OF HONOR

But in a great house there are not only vessels of gold and silver, but also of wood and clay,
some for honor and some for dishonor. Therefore if anyone cleanses himself from the latter, he will be
a vessel for honor, sanctified and useful for the Master, prepared for every good work.

2 TIMOTHY 2:20–24

Watch for a moment the various boats and ships as they glide past on the water. Some are massive, carrying cargo or perhaps part of a military fleet. Others may be sailboats and speedboats, commercial fishing boats, tour boats, even kayaks. Of these vessels, some may gleam with newness and care while others have obviously been around a while. These boats may be made of any number of materials, like wood, fiberglass, or metal. No matter what type of vessel, its age, or what its exterior consists of, we have no idea what's going on inside. It could be carrying passengers, smuggling something sinister, or even both with the former unaware of the latter. We casual spectators can't see inside to know what's taking place.

Similarly, much to our own detriment (and others'), we too could hide our menacing cargo and get away with it . . . for a while. At least long enough to leave a path of destruction. How, then, do we purge the gunk and become a "vessel of honor"? What does that even mean?

Based on Paul's instructions to Timothy, we must remove what's dishonorable in our lives: corrupt influences, false gods and teachings, immoral behavior. This is not saying that we must be perfect and without sin (because none of us is), but we should ask God to point out what needs to go, ask Him for strength to release it, and then be willing to do so. Only then can any of us be a vessel of honor that's useful and prepared. We are to be willing to suffer (Ephesians 3:13); be kind, show respect, put others first (Romans 12:10); and check our motives (James 2:2–4). And ask Him to make use of any past transgressions, either as a lesson for us to learn or to help others (Romans 8:28).

In some respects, all of this may sound counterintuitive when you think about various leaders, coworkers, athletes, artists, and others upon whom honor is bestowed—and in a way it is. We're not promised recognition or reward for our efforts. Not here, anyway. There's no competition for us to win. But if we serve and represent the Master, we cannot do so dishonorably.

Lord, I want to be a vessel that honors You—in my words, in my works, in my daily walk—the way You intended for me to. The phrase "more of You, less of me" applies here. Help me clean out the gunk that's dishonorable in Your eyes and fill my heart with Your truth and love.

SHIP BELLS

Then the LORD God called to Adam and said to him, "Where are you?"

GENESIS 3:9

S ome bells are large enough to be heard from great distances, alerting with intent. Other times, you hear them as you wander among boat slips or harbors, as though the wind gently nudges them awake enough to faintly announce your arrival.

There is a language out on the water that is spoken solely through ship bells.

They are used primarily for communicating through fog. They announce if the vessel is anchored or in trouble, or they simply make a boat's presence known.

Prayer gives us the same vehicle—but, thankfully, our Creator is already in pursuit. Our prayers, we think, send out a signal to let God know how things are going, but, in fact, we have nothing to announce that He is not already aware of. We pray to acknowledge God, petition Him, and, yes, commune with Him.

God pursues us whether we believe Him, believe in Him, or don't believe at all. He desires the connection; we, sometimes unknowingly, are starved for it. Our prayers, then, do not alert Him to *our* presence but, rather, alert us to *His*.

When we become disillusioned and trapped in a fog of sin, we need to sound the alarm. With this in mind, remember that He is always looking for us, searching us out, just as He did with Adam so long ago—no matter how lost we are. Whatever messages we send in our prayers, we have a God who will find us, meet us, and carry us back into His light.

Lord, there are times I cannot see, and I feel lost. I cry out to You; let me feel Your presence. Find me, search me, reveal Yourself to me. I cannot fathom the boundlessness of Your forgiveness and the reasons You pursue me. I am so thankful for Your love.

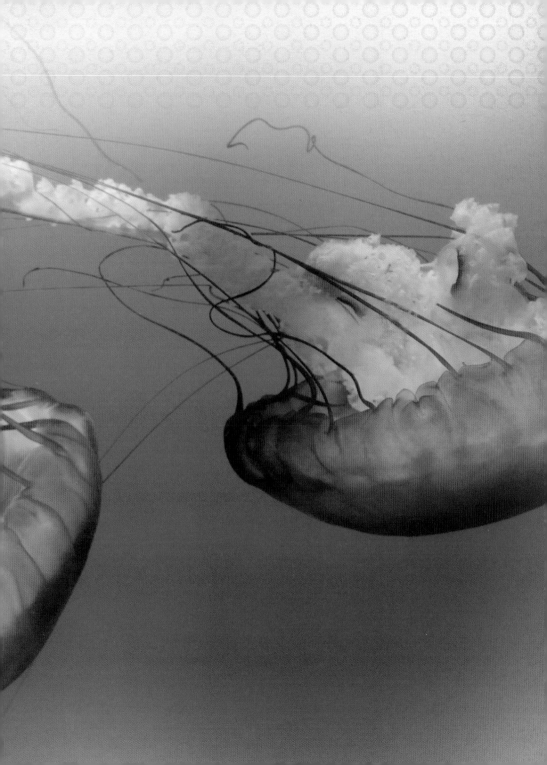

TIDE POOLS

I see God moving across the deserts from Edom,
the Holy One coming from Mount Paran.
His brilliant splendor fills the heavens,
and the earth is filled with his praise.
His coming is as brilliant as the sunrise.
Rays of light flash from his hands,
where his awesome power is hidden.

HABAKKUK 3:3–4 NLT

Tide pools are wondrous things—little microcosms containing scattered bits and pieces of life that have gotten separated from the grand scheme of the ocean. The animals that inhabit them are unable to roam as they once did so they adapt to their smaller, more confined surroundings. And what's interesting is that no tide pool is aware that, maybe just a few inches away, there exists another "world" similar to theirs. More than likely, the organisms in those pools don't know how they got there, but you can be sure they will make the best of the situation in order to survive.

As women, we can get consumed by any number of life's tide pools. Some of us go in willingly, but others of us are trapped before we realize what's happened. Soccer season. School fundraiser. Career. Fitness. Family. Friends. Even church commitments. Any of these sound familiar? We live, breathe, and sleep in these tide pools, often unaware we may be limiting our ability to live fully the way God intended.

There is nothing wrong with staying in our tide pools for a while—sometimes they're for a good cause. But when they consume us and become entrapments, life becomes limited and out of balance. Our energy is then spent trying to survive in the immediate, unable to see, hear, or consider the overall, eternal perspective of life the way the Lord wants us to live it.

What about your tide pools? Is it time to crawl out of one (or several) and get back into experiencing the full scope of living the life God wants for you?

Father God, as I go about my commitments, please keep me from falling prey to settling into routines and going places that cause me to lose sight of You.

TAKING A CLOSER LOOK

"The LORD does not look at the things man looks at.
Man looks at the outward appearance, but the LORD looks at the heart."

I SAMUEL 16:7 NIV

To parody a popular Christmas tune, "It's the most horrible time of the year." In one shopping trip, we go from the window-gazing exclamation, "Oh! That is the cutest swimsuit! I wonder if they have it in my size?" to the dressing-room mirror resignation, "Oh, I look so *awful*!"

Come on, you've been there—agonizing and analyzing while you twist and turn under those horrid fluorescent lights and lamenting that you don't look like the perfect models you see in all the magazines. But the deal is, whatever your reflection looks like, it doesn't tell the whole story about you. Does it describe the kind heart you have, the reliable and faithful friend you are, your generosity toward people in need, or even explain that your tummy protrudes because of surgery? Of course not! It just stares back at you, as you grimace critically.

That's the thing about reflections, whether in the mirror of today or of our pasts; we really need to stop and stare beyond the hardened shell, and go deeper into the soul—our own, as well as others'.

Everyone has a "whole story" to tell. Instead of finding out more about them, however, we tend to grab hold of the first critical thing that bounces off that mirror (our sea of judgment) without taking time to really look into a person's core. At a glance, a neighbor may appear grumpy and unapproachable, but after taking a longer look, you discover he lives in chronic pain and misses his deceased wife. Or that woman who dresses too provocatively at church—from the first time you saw her, you just *knew* she was up to no good. But perhaps after you introduce yourself and eventually invite her for coffee, you discover that she's really very nice and struggles with feeling worthy of God's love, as well as the healthy kind of love she desires from people.

When we consider that others are drawing the same types of conclusions based on our own outward appearances, we should be humbled. From our vantage point, these kinds of assumptions seem unfair. After all, there's so much more to us, right?

But we make these judgments too—and we're the only ones we can change. By taking time to understand why a person is "that way" and extending grace no matter what we may find, we may also unlock a part of ourselves that needs releasing . . . a part that may, in time, emerge as a recognizable part of our own reflections.

Lord, give me a healthy approach to reflection—my own as well as the lives of people You place around me. Help me care for my body as an act of worship and thankfulness, since it is Your creation. Help me care for my soul and spirit by coming to You for healing and growth. When I need to stop and reflect, let me do so without beating myself (or others) up.

COCONUTS

The vessel that he made of clay was marred in the hand of the potter;
so he made it again into another vessel, as it seemed good to the potter to make.

When immersed in seawater, coconuts can survive for several months. Having dropped from the tree, they drift until they are planted or picked up.

Not only does a coconut survive this way, it also survives society's whims. In the 1960s, the coconut was shunned for its fat content. Now, especially with the ramped-up use of coconut water, it's glamorized for its health benefits. Supposedly, about one hundred products can be made from the coconut; every bit of it can be used.

So can we. By God Himself.

Like the coconut, we can drift for a while, but eventually we need to be planted and used. And the Lord can make and remake us over and over again to fit His purposes. Our minds, our hearts, our talents, our physical abilities, even our limitations—He can use them all—to make an impact on this world by bringing clean water to poor countries. God can use us as a friendly face behind a cash register. Or a trusted friend to a teenager. Or a loving home to a stray dog. Or a neighbor who is willing to collect the neighborhood recycling. Or an unexpected meal delivered to a shelter. Or wise counsel to keep an innocent man from going to prison. Or researching a cure for a deadly disease. Or the person who quietly works late to help another meet a deadline. None of these actions is insignificant when prompted by Him.

So, whether you're in a grocery store or on a tropical beach, pick up a coconut and examine it. Consider the many wonders and possibilities contained within—the medicinal properties, the building and landscaping possibilities, even something deliciously fun, like fresh coconut cake. Coconuts are not as pretty or as colorful as, say, the strawberry or lemon, but when shed of its outer core, this hairy, brown fruit can impact millions of lives.

Think about your own talents and abilities and what you'd like to do with them. Then ask God to align your own desires to match His. Ask Him to use every bit of you to accomplish His work. It may be that you smile at strangers or that you reread that report for any overlooked errors, even though you've already read it a million times. Perhaps it's an extra hug for your third child for reasons you cannot explain. Be open to change and flexible enough to be reused and reshaped. The steps may be small or large—but the impact may reverberate for generations.

Lord, I have been drifting in survival mode; I'm ready to be planted. If a single coconut can impact so many, what will You have me do? My heart, mind, and body long to be shaped according to Your purposes, and reshaped as often as needed. Grant me grace to accept if I am to impact only one. It will still make a difference to the life of that person, plant, or animal.

REMAINS OF THE DAYS

Now all these things happened to [our forefathers] as examples,

and they were written for our admonition,

upon whom the ends of the ages have come.

1 CORINTHIANS 10:11

You've been called out of town on business. Pulling a suitcase out of the closet, you unzip it, and a small amount of sand pours out. You sigh, remembering. It was the trip when you tried surfing for the first time, or perhaps the trip when you learned that summer loves rarely last beyond the season, or maybe when you (yikes!) discovered a shellfish allergy. The sand itself didn't teach you these things, but it serves as both a link and a reminder. Sweeping up the remains of your summer, you sigh again, still remembering.

In today's scripture, Paul was not suggesting that we live in the past, but, rather, that we learn from it. Specifically, from Israel's past. The remains, along with the lessons, are chronicled in the Bible so that, centuries later, we can read, believe, learn, and understand. And because the Bible is a living document, we can also *apply*.

Certainly, God speaks to us in other ways, and He has the power to teach us however He deems suitable. But the Bible is a primary, go-to source that offers real-life examples from the lives of others. To a certain extent, we take comfort in knowing that these people weren't so different from us and that, although God warns, commands, and judges, He also still forgives, blesses, comforts, and saves.

Without God's Word, we may never have known that giants roamed the earth (Genesis 6:4). Or that Moses had a speech impediment (Exodus 4:10). Or why Amos was seemingly such an unlikely choice for a prophet (Amos 1:1). Or that Peter, being as gracious as possible, thought of Paul as kind of an egghead (2 Peter 3:15–16). But more importantly are the *lessons* linked to these tidbits.

The people and the events are long gone. What remains not only accounts for history, but also God's purposes and promises. It serves as both a link and a reminder. Why wait for an excuse to open the Bible and to let the lessons pour out? Dive into it regularly *before* a crisis arrives.

Lord, I do not want a Bible that's dusty and untouched. I want a Bible that is worn, frayed, and pliable because I am using it so often. Speak to me as I pore over the words, the passages, the pages. And let the lessons remain long after the Book has closed, never to be swept away from my heart.

VOLCANIC ACTIVITY

"My thoughts are nothing like your thoughts," says the LORD.
"And my ways are far beyond anything you could imagine."
ISAIAH 55:8 NLT

W e have seen the destruction volcanoes can cause as well as the striking
patterns in the landscape after hot lava cools. Did you know, however,
that 90 percent of all volcanic activity occurs in the oceans, mostly unseen by the
casual beachgoer?

Unfortunately, we can approach relationships with the same kind of blindness
as a beachgoer. Our human nature means we are prone to blind spots, particularly
when it comes to people we love. A future husband's free spending habits or seem-
ing lack of patience—these may hardly be noticeable to his loving fiancée, but they
can later reveal an irresponsibility with finances and a harsh temper. That's why
God must sometimes rescue us from our blind spots.

When our hearts are broken, our natural response is to ask *why*. Whether an
eruption in a romantic relationship or a sour ending with someone we thought was
a friend, we must search our own hearts as we ask God where we were blinded. And
thank Him for caring and for loving us enough to spare us from even more hurt.

You see, if we are *truly* seeking God's will for our lives, a breaking point will
occur if a person or situation is not a part of His plan. We may pray, we may cry,
we may even scream at Him—His ways are hard for us to figure out—yet His love
surpasses our understanding. Years later, you may learn the *why* and actually feel
relief that your plans went awry, but some reasons why God does what He does will
not be revealed on this side of heaven. So we must trust that, while we're currently

experiencing the effects of an eruption, God is taking most of the volcanic activity offshore to protect us from something we don't even see.

Lord, You know my heart is broken, and my pain is very real. My plans did not work out despite my best efforts. I want to trust that You have a better plan for me and that I cannot imagine how wonderful that plan is. I am choosing to be hopeful, and I will stay hopeful, because I know that You are faithful and I know that You see what I don't. Open my eyes so that I do not miss Your presence as I journey along the way.

WARNING FLAGS

But if you do warn the righteous man not to sin and he does not sin,
he will surely live because he took warning, and you will have saved yourself.

EZEKIEL 3:21 NIV

Throughout the world, warning flags are found on area beaches. The colors may vary slightly between different beaches, regions, and countries, but the flags are used to warn beachgoers about water, swimming, and weather conditions. Someone is responsible for flying the correct flag for each day's conditions and for remaining watchful so that visitors are able to take proper precautions. The flagmen cannot force individuals to heed the flag's warning; they are simply responsible for delivering the most appropriate message.

Ezekiel shouldered a similar responsibility when God entrusted him to deliver His message to repent. Whether God's people listened or not was not Ezekiel's responsibility—his job was to get the word out. Further along in the story Ezekiel was instructed to do some really odd things and deliver more strong messages, but peppered with all of God's instructions was one final reason behind it all: "then they will know that I am the LORD" (Ezekiel 29:9). Because at some point, for those who did not know, there would be no turning back.

How many of your friends and family are aware you're a practicing Christian? Or do they think you're just a good person? If they know the *who* and the *why* behind your faith and actions, do they see a genuine interest and investment you're making in their lives? Or do they see judgment and legalism?

Think about someone in your life who may not have heard about Christ or does not believe in Christ—someone who could use a friend like Him. Pray about your role in that person's life, for their role in yours, and for the purpose in your paths crossing. Ask the Lord for guidance as you act as His representative. And remember, you can't force on them a relationship with our Savior, but you can certainly make the introduction.

Jesus, who in my life needs to meet You? What do I need to change in my own life to make You visible to others? Do not let me sugarcoat or water down any part of You in my actions and words. Allow me to communicate in ways that will be understood solely by them. Use me however You will so that in this way, they will know You are Lord.

HE'S INTO THE DETAILS

And God said, "Let the water under the sky be gathered to one place, and let dry ground appear."

And it was so. . . . So God created the great creatures of the sea and

every living and moving thing with which the water teems, according to their kinds,

and every winged bird according to its kind. And God saw that it was good.

GENESIS 1:9, 24 NIV

"And God saw that it was good." It sure is—especially when you have an ocean-front view!

Grasp that for a moment. The sea, the sand, the rocks, the birds, the fish, the waves—God made every detail. Every molecule, every grain, every crevice, feather, and gill—He made the entire scene you're taking in. And then, He went even further: He gave us His Son, who provided a way for us to live forever.

Whew! That's a lot to absorb. And it's all nice, and we certainly believe all that, but some of us live on planet earth and have our daily realities to face. Realities like a lost job. Or a broken marriage. Or a failed class. Or a missed opportunity. Or . . . or . . . Yes, God may have provided the way for us to have eternal life, but what about the groceries we need for this week? the unexpected bill that came in the mail? our child's rebellious attitude? those little, day-to-day details that nag and aggravate and weigh us down? How would He have time to deal with that and—better yet—why would He care?

From our vantage points, life can seem overwhelming and even out of control, but He who loves us with a steadfast love is as into the details of our lives as He was when He created the details of bringing together the water and the sandy shores. As

Christ said in Matthew 6:26, the Father knows every bird and He cares for them. How much more He cares for us as His prize creation!

So, have you given your details to God to figure out? Yes, He knows them already, but when we hand them over to Him, something wonderful happens. He arranges them into a bigger picture—with a broader view—to help us work our way out of our futile processes. He's got this plan. It's purposeful. And we may not see the bigger picture as clearly as His oceanfront views, but we can trust that He sees it, and He is working it out. And we'll see that it, too, is good.

Lord, sometimes I forget that while You're "up there," You're also "down here." You know my needs, my cares, my desires—whether it's for wars to end, for a way to pay the orthodontist's bill, or for wisdom in relating to my teenager. Help me release any distrust and doubt, so that I may fully know Your love and care.

HIDING PLACES

They cried to the mountains and the rocks, "Fall on us and hide us from the face

of the one who sits on the throne and from the wrath of the Lamb."

REVELATION 6:16 NLT

Next time you walk along the surf, make a point to look for live sand dollars and little sand crabs. You have to be alert, because they'll scurry back into the sand as quickly as possible, away from your prying eyes.

Oh, how often we try to do that with God. Just like Adam and Eve, we do something or say something that is completely wrong. Really wrong. So wrong we don't recognize ourselves. We know better. We knew better. If we could just run and hide until the big, bad ugliness of it all passes.

We hide ourselves in our charity work, our church obligations, our families. We ignore God; we don't pray. We dismiss His gentle nudge. We're too busy trying to "good" ourselves into acceptance. Or we go into seclusion. Our shame and guilt convince us that we won't recover from that sin. So even at the slightest hint of it emerging and our efforts toward facing it, we keep running, keep trying to hide. Just like those tiny crabs and sand dollars, we want to hide ourselves and our sin from any light that may be shed. It will be too painful, too raw, too much.

Newsflash: it is unlikely that we can escape detection from the Creator of the universe because He created all of our hiding places.

Whatever your sin, your issues, your darkest, most private confessions—bringing them into God's light is the quickest way to move past them and be healed.

You don't have to go public—just go to God. As quickly as you can. Don't scurry and duck like the crabs and sand dollars. That is their means for survival, not yours.

Instead, hide yourself in God's embrace. Envision your face buried in His divine robes, much like a crying child does with a parent. Yes, your heavenly Father already knows, but tell Him anyway. Tell Him what's happened, confess your anguish and sorrow, and ask for forgiveness and grace. Be truly repentant. It's painful, sure, but it is the only, certain way for you to heal.

Abba Father, it's true that I _____. That is a sin in Your eyes, and I come in anguish and sorrow to confess and ask Your forgiveness. I am committed to removing this sin from my life. If there are other actions I need to take—an apology, a declaration, or an elimination—please move me to do so. Thank You, Lord, for the grace You so freely give. May I receive it and not choose to remain ensnared in guilt and shame.

SAND CASTLES

All the Israelite men and women who were willing brought to the Lord freewill offerings
for all the work the Lord through Moses had commanded them to do.

EXODUS 35:29 NIV

Y ou've seen those elaborate sand sculptures—there are contests and even com-
panies that design them. They range from tributes to classical works of art
to favorite cartoon characters. The detail is amazing, and the way the sculptors
embrace their medium is quite remarkable.

There are also those sweet little sand castles built with a child's plastic pail and
shovel. Usually, they amount to a few pail-shaped mounds of sand arranged in a
semicircle, and often left incomplete. There's always one or two mounds that don't
quite embody the pail's shape, and usually you'll find a hole nearby. Or a handmade
mountain made by another child who didn't have the benefit of a pail and shovel.
You can see the little handprints, evidence that eager hands have carefully patted
and packed the sand.

In either case, the artist reaches a point of completion, satisfied that they have
done their best.

Today's scripture refers specifically to the construction of the tabernacle. If you
read the entire chapter, you'll notice that the word *willing* occurs multiple times—
more often than the word *skilled*, which also pops up more than once. As Moses
delivered God's instructions to the people of Israel, we learn that their skills varied
among them. Because the word *willing* becomes more and more dominant as the
chapter progresses, two questions come to mind:

1. Were some who either were skilled or had the means unwilling?
2. In terms of service, is it more important to be willing or skilled?

The Lord is concerned that we try our best in all our tasks. Whether we are sewing on a button or running a Fortune 500 company, the quality of our work should be a testament to the abilities and talents God has given us. The passion and willingness, however, cannot be overlooked. As believers, that attitude, that energy, is just as integral to the work itself.

For the Israelites, the combination of the two—along with a cooperative, community effort—built a tabernacle. Sand sculptors of all ages build castles. What are you building?

Lord, help me explore further the talents and abilities You have entrusted to me. Open my eyes to opportunities You've provided, that I may use these gifts to Your glory. If I build small or large, that is Your decision. Just enable my mind and heart to be willing to build for You.

BOARDWALKS AND
BEACH CARNIVALS

The whole law can be summed up in this one command:
"Love your neighbor as yourself."
But if you are always biting and devouring one another, watch out!
Beware of destroying one another.

GALATIANS 5:14–15 NLT

A h, boardwalks and beach carnivals—eroding, yet delightful eyesores on coast-al landscapes everywhere. Sickly, humming yellow lights, dingy structures, an odd menagerie of people, cheap tchotchkes, and gastrointestinal nightmares, all with a backdrop of happy shrieks and music that usually ranges from tired and sagging to just plain off-key. In addition to lacking in eye appeal, parts of these fun zones are weird. As children, we found them exciting and fun, but as adults, we don't want to touch anything or talk to anyone.

Often, we view churches and ministries with the same critical lens.

The people are weird, the music may not suit our tastes, the facilities and re-sources aren't pristine, and the covered-dish suppers turn into tummyaches. As children, we may have loved church, but now it doesn't meet our expectations and standards. Maybe God's people let you down in some way; maybe you simply lost interest; maybe it's just easier to dismiss the soloist with tangerine hair and heavy blue eyeshadow who can't sing than it would be to get to know her heart.

There are valid reasons for leaving a church or a particular ministry. It's also true that no church is perfect. But when we criticize our own churches and other

Lord, thank You for providing so many reminders in Your creation that parallel Your love, our journey, and Your provision. Keep my faith like those swimming toward a sandbar they do not see—keep me bold, keep me certain, and keep me willing. Help me grow in each of these areas, making me a stronger swimmer as I move closer and closer to You.

PELICANS

So [Elijah] said, "I have been very zealous for the LORD God of hosts;
for the children of Israel have forsaken Your covenant,
torn down Your altars, and killed Your prophets with the sword.
I alone am left; and they seek to take my life."

1 KINGS 19:10

White pelicans are fairly lone creatures, due in part to the way they must drain their pouches after catching fish. The process can take up to a minute, giving other sea birds plenty of time to steal the pelican's food from its mouth. These uninvited dinner guests will take every last morsel from their host, so it's no wonder white pelicans prefer to dine alone.

Do you identify with the pelican? Does it seem like the world just takes and takes, leaving you to starve mentally or emotionally? In some ways, you are no longer fed? Maybe it's your family, friends, work, church commitments, even social engagements . . . or all of the above. No one seems willing to step up and help, and you're alone in the chaos of it all. Okay, but some of it may be self-created.

Elijah was frustrated with God's people and ready to give up. The Lord pursued, asking him why he fled. Elijah's response was to talk about all that he'd done for God—or not done against Him—and that he was the only righteous man left. The last man standing.

Now, keep in mind that Elijah chose a life of isolation. Fleeing to the desert was just a geographical form of it. And by doing so, he was abandoning those who were faithful and supportive, even if they were outnumbered by the wicked and corrupt.

In all fairness, Elijah's life was, indeed, threatened, but he'd left those who were counting on him.

If you're familiar with the story, you know that God directed Elijah to stand in His presence. God then sent great winds and hurricanes, but Elijah did not find God in the calamity. He was found in the very small voice that followed. The voice directed Elijah to go back and enlist help.

God knew Elijah was worn out, and He knows you are too. But we are to honor our commitments unless He directs otherwise. You won't find answers in the calamity and chaos. Listen instead for the still, small voice that may be telling you to go back and enlist help.

Lord, when it comes to _____, I have been feeling like that pelican. I'm trying to do what I think is best, but it's never good enough nor quick enough. It seems like everyone wants to just take from me without any regard for whether it's right or fair. Give me strength to confront them and humility to enlist help. And, Lord, I release all of this to You. So I ask for discernment, should Your answer be that someone else needs to take this mantle from me.

COOKOUTS

Jesus answered and said to her,
"Martha, Martha, you are worried and troubled about many things.
But one thing is needed, and Mary has chosen that good part,
which will not be taken away from her."

LUKE 10:41-42

What is it about the beach cookout that makes food taste better, whether it be hamburgers, hotdogs, seafood, or even five loaves of bread and two fish! The more impromptu, the better. Everyone brings what they have, pitch it all in, and it's a party. New friends are made as more people are . . . well, for lack of a better way of putting it, drawn to the flames. We eat, we play. Eventually, someone locates a guitar and softly plays while we, feeling full and snuggled in, watch the flames and listen to the music until embers close down a lovely day.

Would we dare entertain this way at home? Would we—with piles of laundry waiting on us—fire up our grills and spontaneously invite a few friends or neighbors over? Or make five quarts of chili and, as it cooks, invite others over to watch a football game? Or do we wait and plan for the perfect moment, the perfect time, and the perfect setting to display our single-minded *wow* factor?

In some respects, *hospitality* has been narrowly defined in recent years, thanks to the age of tablescapes and celebrity chefs. But as we can see from today's scripture, this narrow perspective isn't a new concept. Many of us feel sorry for Martha. She was trying to present her best, go the extra mile, pull out all the stops for Jesus. Wouldn't we do the same if we knew He were coming? There'd be no wienie roast for Him!

But Jesus *is* in our homes every day; yet, we're so busy with all of our tasks, many days we miss "that good part." And when we invite others into our home, we're so busy making sure everything is perfect, we miss "that good part" with them too.

Of course, it's fun to throw a grand dinner or lavish party with all of the details executed perfectly, but don't lose sight of why you're doing it. Don't miss enjoying the people you're honoring or the investment of personal time with them because you've opted to serve beef tenderloin instead of throwing a few burgers on the grill. (If you don't cook, just know the former requires more attention than the latter!)

Think back to how satisfying that beach cookout feels. Invite a friend over for morning coffee instead of brunch. Or let the laundry wait so you can spend more time in prayer. It's not as easy as it sounds, but sometimes we have to peel away the trappings in order to get to "that good part."

Lord, help me be more spontaneous about how I invest in the lives of others and how I spend time with You. Remind me that the "perfect time" isn't always apparent, but can be quite rewarding.

SINCERITY OF HEART

The LORD does not see as man sees;
for man looks at the outward appearance,
but the LORD looks at the heart.

1 SAMUEL 16:7

If you've ever visited the Atlantic Ocean during the summer, you probably enjoyed its inviting warmth, spectacular color, gentle waves, and endless horizon. And if you've ever visited Antarctica (even if only in photographs), you probably experienced below freezing temperatures, a colorless view, and an endless expanse of ice. These contrasting scenes make an interesting point about God's people.

There are mature believers who quietly carry out the Lord's work without much fanfare or attention-getting. Our spirit tells us that *something* about them is different, even if they've never discussed their faith. But sometimes their quietness makes their faith hard to read and can lead to uncertainty in our relationship.

Then there are those believers who are very vocal about Jesus: they don't shy away at all from bringing Him up or quoting His Word in conversations. Sometimes these outspoken followers may not be as warm and approachable as the quieter believer, but there's no doubt where they stand on spiritual matters.

Whether His child is clearly one style or the other, or somewhere in between, God knows each and every human heart. While some of His children may be soft-spoken, that doesn't mean they have *less* faith. At the same time, the more vocal believer doesn't necessarily have *more*. Besides, we need both types of believers in our journey.

We cannot judge another person's heart or the sincerity of her faith—and we don't need to! What's most important to remember is that penguins thrive in Antarctica, while sea turtles flourish in the Atlantic—and the differences are good!

Lord, when I feel frustrated with other believers—with either their almost overpowering display of devotion to You or their perceived lack of enthusiasm for what Jesus did on the cross for them—help me remember that I am not to judge.

PLOUGH MUD

Though the fig tree does not bud
and there are no grapes on the vines,
though the olive crop fails
and the fields produce no food,
though there are no sheep in the pen
and no cattle in the stalls,
yet I will rejoice in the LORD,
I will be joyful in God my Savior.
The Sovereign LORD *is my strength;*
He makes my feet like the feet of a deer,
He enables me to go on the heights.

HABAKKUK 3:17–19 NIV

I t has a smell unlike any other—a mixture of soil, decay, and sand; a mixture of past and present, if you will. It isn't quicksand, though for the many shoes lost, there is no difference. They suffer the same fate in the suction.

Plough mud is incredibly soft. It houses plants and animals, dead and alive. If you're not familiar with it and happen to step in it, it's too late. You're stuck. You'll slosh along, slower and slower, each step sucking your feet or shoes deeper and deeper into it. You'll hear its sighs and gasps as you pull and strain to keep moving.

Our faith can get like that too. There are simply those times when our faith becomes stuck. We're convinced there's a black cloud following us around. We're ready to give up. What's the point, after all?

Our lives feel stalled. We are alone in this big, bad world while everyone else has direction. Even if their direction isn't a path we'd choose, at least they're moving. They're on a path. We're just sitting. And waiting. Stuck in the stinky mud. No one helps. We have nowhere to turn. We're just stuck. Where is God?

He is working, my dear, and you need to stop thinking He isn't. Remember the fig tree that bears no fruit, or the vineyard in the same situation. Trees look positively dead in the winter then bud in the spring, right?

When you're stuck, stalled, or even stale, stay faithful . . . even when life feels empty. Pray honestly and earnestly. Enlist others to pray. Remind yourself of joys past, trusting your joy will again return. God has plans that will not leave you stuck in the mud. As verse 19 says, the Lord is sovereign and will eventually give you "the feet of a deer" to get on higher, more stable ground.

Lord, I am weary. I pull, strain, sigh, and gasp my way along until I feel like I can move no longer. I am stuck. I renew my choice to believe that You are at work. If the tree buds and the tulips return in the spring, my faith will dislodge from the sticky mud and burst through with new growth too. Spiritual pruning is painful, but purposeful, and I will trust Your ways.

TIES THAT BIND

He gives strength to the weary
and increases the power of the weak.
Even youths grow tired and weary,
and young men stumble and fall;
but those who hope in the LORD
will renew their strength.

ISAIAH 40:29–31 NIV

W ander by an old dock or around some boat slips, and you'll hear the muffled, rythmic moans of ropes, indicative of pain, of tension, of the purposeful intent to hang on. Whether they're holding a boat in place, collecting a fresh catch of shrimp, or serving as a safety railing for onlookers, a rope cannot deviate from its intended purpose without devastating consequences. Its rest is reserved for another time.

Now move in closer and study those ropes. You'll notice that time and tension also contribute to their frayed, discolored appearance. Ironically, however, these alleged blemishes make them more pliable, more useful, and even stronger . . . until, with every fiber spent, their work is completed and they can do no more.

How many days do you experience something similar? You are quietly straining, moaning, painfully trying to keep it together for the sake of others, and maybe unsure that you can. The wearied tension is there, but the respite isn't. You bear the marks of time and experience, but don't seem to gain the wisdom and strength.

Quite often, our pain has purpose; but just as often, we don't see it. Instead, we focus on the fear of what might happen if our grip should slip.

The difference is, however, that even if we let go, God hasn't let go of us. He doesn't. And He won't.

There are times when we can't hang on with our own strength, and other times when there wouldn't be much point in doing so. It's then that we have a choice: stay coiled up, pristine, and remain useless; cling so tightly to what is familiar and be so stressed by our fear of the unknown that we snap; or yield to what God would have us do, even if that means letting go.

And having faith that He hasn't. He doesn't. And He won't.

Father, give me discernment to know the difference between purposeful pain and paralyzing fear. Make my heart and spirit pliable enough to receive Your divine instruction and faith that enables me to hold tight or let go, trusting Your perfect guidance.

HIGH TIDE, LOW TIDE, EBB TIDE

But I keep praying to you, LORD,
hoping this time you will show me favor.
In your unfailing love, O God,
answer my prayer with your sure salvation.

PSALM 69:13 NLT

bb tide describes the outgoing tide—the period between high tide and low. Sometimes you'll hear it described as "falling tide."

As women, our ebb tides can be almost worse than our low tides. That stumbling, receding, reversal of fortune—any sort of fortune—can eat us alive, stripping us of security, joy, peace. Even dignity. And sometimes hope.

For us, it may be the late notices on bills you cannot pay. The husband who seems distant. The announcement that confirms layoffs are pending. The wait to find out if the child you're carrying has a serious health condition. We cannot get resolution and we don't know whether to move forward or sideways. We're caught.

Sometimes these events unfold because of our bad decisions. Sometimes, they have nothing to do with anything we've done. Regardless, we reach the point where we finally understand we are not in control—and we never were. So we wait, not knowing how much more uncertainty awaits, and we play through our minds how we'll respond whenever a breakthrough finally happens.

Almost anything can trigger our ebb tide, but once we realize we're on it, the agony of the trip spins us into worry, depression, and the constant thought of *When will this end?*

Scripture catches David in a similar place. He was the object of ridicule and scorn. Whispers about his activities abounded, with added embellishment and lies. But he waited and stayed faithful, knowing that God's "acceptable time" would deliver him.

When you find yourself being swept into the ebb tide, remember David's prayer. Pray for God's "acceptable" timing, whether His provision comes in the form of a miraculous, immediate rescue, or as a means for seeing you through. And remember, the tide *will* rise again to take you safely back to shore.

Father, thank You for David's reminder that we are ultimately not in control and we should call out to You in hopeless situations. Let me not forget to praise You in times of plenty, but I shall also praise You during times of lack and uncertainty—for all of these draw me closer to You. Thank You for Your provision and mercy.

SEA GLASS

And we know that in all things God works for the good of those who love him,
who have been called according to his purpose.

ROMANS 8:28 NIV

People collect sea glass for a variety of reasons: to occupy the time of a restless child, to make jewelry or art, or simply because they like it. The colors are beautiful and varied. It's a fun way to spend time at the beach, and some colors, such as pale pink or green, are considered quite rare.

Have you ever considered its humble beginnings? All of it starts as glass that has been thrown away, discarded, and broken. Pieces of a former whole no longer serves their intended purpose, so they are cast away—then tossed about, taking some hard knocks, and finally, emerging smooth, refined, beautiful. And pursued by someone who has a different purpose in mind.

Likewise, there are those days, even seasons, when we feel fragmented and useless. Or discarded and forgotten. By friends who don't return calls, promotions that pass us by, children who take us for granted, husbands whose presence is more like a vapor in our homes. Parts of a former whole, we find ourselves being tossed about, taking hard knocks, unsure of our direction or purpose.

All the while, however, we *are* being pursued. By One who has a different purpose in mind.

The Father knows, and sometimes orchestrates, our seasons of refinement—it is part of a greater plan, His plan, which serves His purposes. These are not necessarily fun times—even for believers who know this—to ask, "Why me?" or to declare, "Not again!" is only human. Even when we're on the other side of that season, we may still not understand fully the *why* behind it, but we can be sure we have a Father who loves us, pursues us, and—once His hand is upon us—does not let go.

Trust that during these seasons, we are being refined and transformed into something useful. And ultimately, beautiful.

Lord, I feel empty and useless. Am I forgotten? Am I unloved? Renew my trust that You are always at work, even during the times I don't see it and I don't feel it. Speak to me in ways that are personal and intimate—ways I know it's You speaking. Remind me that, even in this season, I am part of a much bigger plan—that's how important I am to You. I'd rather feel dormant and be used by You than actively used by anyone else for a purpose that was not Yours.

LEANING PALM TREES

For God, who said, "Let light shine out of darkness," made his light shine in our hearts
to give us the light of the knowledge of the glory of God in the face of Christ.

2 CORINTHIANS 4:6 NIV

Have you ever noticed how a palm tree's trunk curves and leans? Most appear to lean toward the ocean, but did you know it's not for nourishment from the water? They're actually leaning toward another life source: the light.

The scientific term for this is *phototropism*, and since more light reflects back from the sea, the trees naturally reach for as much light as possible. Interestingly enough, leaning this way makes it easier for them to reproduce successfully, since the current can carry their seeds away for dispersal.

That's got gospel written all over it! As believers, our spiritual depth and breadth take a similar approach; we are a seed planted by a current of fellow believers who reflect light and help us grow. As we grow, we lean toward (or on) this same community to, in fact, reach for more of our true life Source: the light of our Lord. And in His timing, our own seeds are planted and carried to other places to renew the process.

The light itself is essential for the one tree's survival; seed dispersal is essential for that of its species. How many times in our own leanings do we mistake the community for the Source? Or are reluctant to plant any seeds?

Lord Jesus, thank You for the graceful reminder of who You are, who I am, and what we're supposed to be, so artfully depicted in the lovely image of a palm tree. Let me also reflect on how it moves in the breeze, bends in a storm, and always, always, leans back toward the light.

JELLYFISH

"O Death, where is your sting?
O Hades, where is your victory?"
The sting of death is sin, and the strength of sin is the law.
But thanks be to God,
who gives us the victory through our Lord Jesus Christ.

1 CORINTHIANS 15:55-57

O uch. Ouch. OUCH! Jellyfish stings are the *worst*. How can something so graceful and unusual-looking pack such a horrible punch? What did we ever do to them?

And the thing is, once we're stung, if we try to remove the tentacles ourselves, more venom is released! Some jellyfish stings may be treated with vinegar, but vinegar aggravates other types of jellyfish stings. The little beasts don't give us a way out without proper assistance. The pain can last anywhere from a few minutes to a few weeks. Thankfully, it's not forever.

And neither is death. Not for believers, anyway. But we have days where we need reassurance. Believers in Corinth were in the same position.

To be frank, this is one of those chapters where we wonder if Paul would have made a great captain for his high school debate team. As he argued against the assertion that Jesus rose from the dead—a position many believers and nonbelievers still take today—our brains start to hurt, but there is a method to Paul's approach. By starting there, he could use their logic to, ironically enough, reduce their argument to its nonsensical core. If Christ hasn't risen, there was no point to the Christian faith nor His work. He'd be better off keeping his mouth shut and making tents, building a prosperous life for himself.

Paul didn't just make tents, though, because the bodily resurrection of Jesus actually happened. Which means that death could not contain Him—and by His proxy, death will not contain us. Whether death comes swiftly or slowly creeps up on us, we will not be stung by death, thanks to Jesus' victory. His death and resurrection were one-time events, and they are effective throughout all time. It was a once, and it was for all.

Lord Jesus, thanks to You, I have conquered death! Your resurrection took care of it, and I need not fear it. And when I grieve for loved ones who go before me, gently remind me that death did not conquer them either, and that our separation is only for a short time.

CLEAR NIGHTS

Then God made two great lights: the greater light to rule the day,

and the lesser light to rule the night. He made the stars also.

W ander down to the beach on a clear night, just as you have done during the day. Lie down, stretch out on your back, and stare straight up into the enormity of the sky. It seems bigger, doesn't it? Now lose yourself in the vastness of the stars. Can you help but wonder, *What have they witnessed?*

Very few components of our world existed before the stars: Earth. Sky. Heaven. Water. Land. Trees and grass. The stars bore witness to just about all that followed: Animals. Man. The Fall. Moses parting the Red Sea. David and Bathsheba. Elizabeth's and Mary's pregnancies. The birth and resurrection of Christ. Mary and Martha hosting Jesus and the disciples. Paul on the road to Damascus. Joan of Arc. The signing of the Declaration of Independence. The first space flight. Your birth. What you did yesterday. How you are spending today.

David wrote about this idea in the 19th Psalm, which opens with, "The heavens declare the glory of God." God reveals Himself to us any number of ways, but truly, in nature, we see His power and creativity. The stars have been there throughout history, dedicated by God to provide "signs" (Genesis 1:14) and indications of seasons. The arrangement of the stars is not random. Over the centuries, they have helped sailors and awed scientists with their order. All of our plans, actions, and schemes have taken place under the stars' watchful eyes, but they are there to declare God's glory. Are we paying the kind of attention this part of creation deserves from us?

The stars have been here almost from the beginning. And they will remain after we're gone. In the meantime, they bear witness to what they've seen and what they know by declaring God's glory. In our meantime, so should we.

Father, I look at the night sky with awe. What a beautiful display for those of us who take the time to look! I thank You for such beauty as the stars truly declare Your glory. They remind me that I am to do the same.

REFLECTIONS

Ca-lunka, calunka-lunka-lunk . . . caaa-lunka, calunka-lunka-lunk . . .
Weighted down by your children's beach accessories and your own sweat,
you and your husband amble awkwardly to your perfect beach spot and plant the
flag . . . or the umbrella, in this case. The noise and calamity surrounding your arrival has caused a disturbance. You just know everyone is annoyed and staring. Fine,
you think. *Let 'em stare.*

Your white, pasty skin will blind some of them, and the rest of them will
lose their appetites just looking at you in your at-least-it-fits swimsuit. "Wake me
when lunch is ready," your husband yawns, as you notice that the hair on his back
is graying.

Between performing the seated shimmy out of your full-body swimsuit cov-
er-up and planking to soak up a few rays, you take a moment to sigh wistfully at
the teens playing keep-away nearby. Two of the players are young girls, shrieking
gleefully in their little daisy-print and polka-dotted bikinis while boys pretend to
tackle them, only to laugh and swing them around as if they are weightless. You
sigh again, while your husband snores and your youngest is already bugging you
for a juicebox.

Somewhere else, on that same beach, another woman sits with her husband,
grieving her second miscarriage. She watches you wistfully, wanting a child to
bother her for a juicebox. And another woman watches this couple over her book,
unaware of their grief. She is longing, instead, for a companion who would rub her

arm and kiss her cheek the way this woman's husband does. And of course, someone else notices *her*, and envies the delicious simplicity of this woman's solitude. The stares and the longings continue, each woman viewing another's reflection and thinking it's her own. Or should be.

Reflections don't tell the entire story.

Setting our own standards based on someone else's reflection won't firm your flabby thighs, nor take away that post-baby weight that you're still carrying . . . four years later. Yet, we stare at various pieces of other people's lives and think their journey should be our own. We somehow lose sight that God made us all in His image, but each one of us is truly a one-of-a-kind design. So while we could never be them, *nor can they be us*.

In Ecclesiastes 9, Solomon wrote about these same kinds of inequalities and the unfairness in life—and wasn't he the guy who had it all? He surmised that what we have or don't have won't add a moment to our lives. Therefore, he concluded, we are to make the most of our time, because "even a live dog is better off than a dead lion!" (v. 4b NIV).

Just as the song says, we are precious in His sight. For today, rest in this. Then try again tomorrow.

Lord, forgive me for all the ways I look at others and compare. I am me. There is no other me in this world. Guide me to be the me You intended. And as You do, may I find true contentment with who You created.

PENGUINS

Teach us to number our days aright,
that we may gain a heart of wisdom.

PSALM 90:12 NIV

It is unlikely that you would head to the beaches of Antarctica for rest, relaxation, and rejuvenation. But don't totally dismiss that cold continent. We can learn important lessons from the creatures that do spend time there, including various species of penguins.

Compare, for instance, their on-land abilities and their water skills:

* On land, penguins have no predators and therefore are generally unafraid of humans. The penguins' natural enemies primarily lurk in the water.
* On land, penguins move slowly, with a distinct and silly waddle. Once in the water, however, penguins can "fly" up to 25 miles per hour.
* On land, penguins are quite nearsighted, but their vision in the water is keen and clear.

A believer can learn much from these basic penguin facts.

In the water, these cartoonish birds are transformed from nearsighted and sluggish to sharp-eyed and fast. So why don't they simply remain in the water? Penguins are in the water for about 75 percent of their lives, but the icy Antarctic beaches are key to their survival. You see, most of the seventeen known species that live in Antarctica have rookeries on shore where they waddle to breed, rest, and sometimes feed.

When we seek and find our God-ordained work—whether for a season or a lifetime—He gives us not only great vision, but also the ability to soar. But during other seasons of life, we feel as if we're waddling across a seemingly barren place. If we take a cue from our arctic friends, at these times we need to seek counsel and comfort from others, to be fed, to rest, and to accept that it's not yet time for us to swim once again.

And just like the penguin, we need not be fearful during those times. While we have many would-be predators in our waddling as well as our soaring seasons, we do not have to live in fear of them . . . because we know who is with us. And He is all-powerful.

Father, help me remember the penguins on their icy beach when my life seems stalled and uncertain. Remind me that time on this beach is a necessary part of life. Help me remember to use those times to regroup, refresh, and reconnect with You.

HAMMOCKS

Walk worthy of the calling . . . with all lowliness and gentleness,
with longsuffering, bearing with one another in love,
endeavoring to keep the unity of the Spirit in the bond of peace.

EPHESIANS 4:1–3

Rock steady. Rock, rock, rock. Rock steady.

It's not an easy entry, but once you've landed in a hammock, the gentle rocking motion takes you back to infancy. By design, mobility in a hammock is somewhat limited, but that doesn't matter—you are cradled in safety. The fibers are bound, connected, and tied, and their common purpose supports and protects. Their strength is best demonstrated in the stress and tension.

You already see where this is going, don't you?

Believers disagree on many matters. Worship styles. Color of new sanctuary carpet. Politics. Social justice. Youth ministries. Soloists. Parenting. Instruments. Environmental issues. Lifestyles. Money. Current events. News sources. Biblical interpretation. The list is long and the degree of disagreement is broad. After all, we are not mass produced. But we have something in common that should supersede any and all disagreements: Christ.

Somehow, we not only have to bridge the gaps of our disagreements and grumblings, but we have to find a way to bond, connect, and tie ourselves together with fellow believers if we, as a body, are to be effective.

This call to unity doesn't apply solely in church situations; it applies to our relationships with all believers. The coworker who clears his throat a thousand times a day. The annoying neighbor who smugly refers to your church as "a little too loosey-goosey" for her taste. The sorority sister who dates your ex-boyfriend (not something you wanted to have in common with her!). The boss who "gave" you a forced retirement. We have to reach down deep and find that, er, *special godly love* for those who cannot be accommodated with the human "like" button. Paul referred to it more eloquently as "endeavoring to keep the unity of the Spirit in the bond of peace."

And it's not up to you to determine if they are willing to do the same. In those cases, as many people often say, just "let God do."

But when the "endeavoring" actually occurs among God's people, the uncertain seeker is enticed. Like climbing into a hammock, the entry into a circle of believers may be somewhat awkward. There may be some back-and-forth sway, but the support will be there, and seekers will discover who it is they've been seeking. Paying careful attention to the bonds, connections, and close ties, they will see how the group's strength is demonstrated best when tension is present, and they will feel cradled in the secure comfort of a body that rocks steady, because it is anchored by One who cares for every strand.

Father, as I think about fellow believers who just plain irritate me or even make me angry because they constantly disagree, I struggle to be nice—because I really don't want to be. I wrestle with this, because I am reminded that You made them too. You love them too. How do I go about loving them without just faking it? That's where I am, Lord. Help me see them as You do.

SHUCKING OYSTERS:
GOD PRIES OUR HEARTS

But will God really dwell on earth?
The heavens, even the highest heaven, cannot contain you.
How much less this temple I have built!

1 KINGS 8:27 NIV

Carefully, the tip of your knife pierces, then wiggles into the hinge. Sometimes, they can be stubborn, and the knife can slip—and since the shell is sharp, your hands are vulnerable. When you finally hear that first little pop, your knife goes in, staying careful to remain near the top of the shell so as not to slice the oyster that's inside.

Fresh oysters are a big treat—but you have to work at them a little. Shucking them can be tricky because they're not very eager to be opened. You're essentially prying them at your own risk. But how lovely to discover what's inside!

Our hearts are much like that oyster shell, particularly if we've experienced great pain or loss. The shell protecting a wounded heart remains sealed, hardened, sharp, protecting the fragile softness inside.

We become so hardened that we close our hearts even to God. But God, our God, who cannot be contained, certainly has the power to blast open our hearts if He so chooses. So we're kidding ourselves to think we can truly keep Him away. We're only able to shut Him out because of the free will that He provided.

Now, consider that out of all the places in the world He could reside, He desires your heart. Your broken, sharp-edged, hardened heart. He wants to live there.

Incidentally, a beautiful pearl forms when something slips between the mantle and shell of an oyster. Consider what treasures God may create if He has the same access into your heart.

Lord, parts of my heart are hard and closed and brittle. I have closed them to my own detriment. The fear of opening them again is a painful thought, but I trust that You will handle tenderly the softness that's inside. Thank You for not forcing me; thank You for loving me enough to not forsake me. Thank You that, You are willing to enter even a heart as hard as mine, willing to dwell there, and willing to build.

THE PERFECT BEACH TRIP

He who observes the wind will not sow,
And he who regards the clouds will not reap.
As you do not know what is the way of the wind,
Or how the bones grow in the womb of her who is with child,
So you do not know the works of God who makes everything.

ECCLESIASTES 11:4–5

How many times have you had the "perfect" beach trip? (Hmmm . . . really, is there any other kind?)

Well, there was that time it rained. Or the time you tried a new beach house and got lost for two hours trying to find it. Or the time your toddler got an ear infection the first full day you were there. Or the toilet in your rental didn't work right. Or . . .

Okay, okay. So maybe at the point-by-point level, you've never had a perfect beach trip. So how did you deal with the bumps in the road? Did you manage to make the most of the situation, or did you let it ruin your trip?

There are those times we just want—even demand—perfection in order to execute our plans. Planning a wedding. Planning to exercise. Planning a quiet time. The conditions have to be perfect for us to act, or we give up because it's utterly ruined. Planning, planning, waiting, waiting . . . the moment has to be exactly right.

And, to be fair, planning and preparation are important. But if we spend our time waiting for perfect conditions, we're actually wasting our time. The perfection is simply not gonna happen.

Sometimes we have to simply act and trust God for the next step. If we make a wrong turn because we misunderstood the Holy Spirit, then we trust that the Father will correct our steps. If we make a wrong decision because we ignored Him, we confess our neglect and trust Him for the next step. And there are times He will wait until we act—because growing our trust is far more important than our knowing the end result. We belong to God: our relationship with Him is assured through the blood of Jesus Christ. So if you look ridiculous, are made fun of, or appear to have failed at something that you've prayerfully considered—do not fear. Trust God with His timing.

Our time here on Earth is finite. And none of its days is perfect. There are only so many days we'll spend here—waiting on the perfect one sure seems like a futile way to spend them.

Lord, remind me that if I'm waiting for a perfect moment, that waiting may be rooted in fear. As Your child and Your creation, I will never be a failure, regardless of what the world sees and thinks. Sometimes my own plans will fail, but in a way only known to You, they are still successful—because You remain sovereign. Let this truth give me wings and a willingness to take risks, take chances, and never fear failure. I am grateful and thankful to You always, in all situations. What a great gift it is to take refuge in You!

Riptides

When they heard that he spoke to them in
the Hebrew language, they kept all the more silent.

Acts 22:2

Riptides—or, more accurately, rip currents—are strong, narrow currents that occur when water that's been trapped between an underwater sand bar and the shore gives way and pushes back out to sea. Swimmers are warned about the dangers riptides pose. They are cautioned not to go with their natural instinct—that is, to fight to swim back to shore—but rather to swim parallel to the shore to get out of the current and then swim back to shore and to safety.

Paul was caught in a verbal riptide. He'd been attacked for blasphemy and defiling the temple with Gentiles. The Roman commander saw the uproar and had Paul arrested. In the previous chapter, he had arrested Paul first and asked questions later (Acts 24:33). Ironically enough, had Paul not been arrested, he would have been beaten to death by Jews very fervent for God.

Paul was basically getting it from all sides. Was he Egyptian? Was he Greek? Was he Roman? Was he a Jew? Just who was this troublemaker?

Only the Holy Spirit could have used parts and pieces of "Saul" to equip Paul with the proper response.

Initially mistaken by the commander for an Egyptian wanted for causing a riot, Paul spoke Greek to him, indicating he was not only well educated, but also well versed in the culture and not someone looking to riot. This indicator paved way for him to address the crowd, which he did in Hebrew, to let them know he was a devout Jew with established credentials. Later in chapter 22, Paul's life was spared once again when he reminded them that he was a natural-born Roman citizen—he did not pay for it—and therefore could not be flogged without proof of guilt.

Navigating the riptides as he did, Paul "swam" parallel with the shore until he could find a way into the hearts and minds of those who might not otherwise listen to him. He spoke their languages, he reminded them of what they themselves stood for, and he worked until he found common ground from which he could deliver his message.

How do you handle the riptides of those who do not believe? Do you continue to swim in shallow, safe waters—or do you dare venture out, knowing that you may encounter people who challenge or defy what you stand for? And when you do encounter them, what is your response? Do you fight and attempt to overtake the current, which is the natural response? Or do you give in? Or . . . do you swim parallel, forming an authentic relationship, and finding common ground that will lead to the revelation of Truth?

Holy Spirit, I ask you to use the parts and pieces of my "Saul" to equip me with my "Paul." Give me the courage to venture out and handle the riptides as they come, with the wisdom, deed, and words You provide.

FROM SWEET TO STENCH

Restore to me the joy of your salvation and
grant me a willing spirit, to sustain me.

PSALM 51:12 NIV

Freshness, at the beach, is fleeting. Fresh seafood, wet swimsuits, even seashells can rot, decay, and mildew in short order without proper, immediate care. Very quickly, the sweetness of fresh air erodes into a stench. Our spirits can suffer the same fate.

Being spirit-filled—Holy Spirit-filled—requires frequent replenishment to stay fresh. For some of us, it's a daily requirement; for others, it may even be hourly. Regardless of our reasons—perhaps we disregard God or forget about Him, or maybe we think He's forgotten about us—we have moments when we do not approach the throne. These moments can stem from overconfidence in our successes or from dark, depressing situations. We neglect a very specific need when we ignore our spiritual gas tanks. This is what happened with David.

David was riding high. He was a successful leader, he enjoyed communion with the Lord, and then, for a moment, he was distracted. That's all it took for temptation to put a stench on his spirit and his life. It took Nathan, the brave prophet and David's friend, confronting David and forcing him to examine the destruction he'd created by one moment's distraction.

But David loved God, and he knew that He had the power to restore him, something David himself couldn't accomplish by winning wars or wooing women. So David asked God for "a willing spirit"—that is, a heart soft and open to hearing, and more importantly, obeying God's commands, because that is what would get him through, regardless of his circumstances. David's sin forever altered the course of his life and the lives of his descendants, but God forgave him for his sin, which was far more valuable than his getting off the hook in his immediate situation.

David saw the direct connection between a willing spirit and sustainability. The renewal of David's spirit could be preserved through God's power as well as through his own willingness to be renewed and filled as often as possible with that power.

Could your spirit use a little refreshment today?

Lord, just as David asked so long ago, I ask You now to replenish and refresh my spirit. Fill me with Your power and Your wisdom, keep my heart open and willing to receive Your power at any moment. This is how I will be sustained by You.

NETS

When [the net] was full, the fishermen pulled it up on the shore.
Then they sat down and collected the good fish in baskets,
but threw the bad away. This is how it will be at the end of the age.
The angels will come and separate the wicked from the righteous.

MATTHEW 13:48–49 NIV

Have you ever watched how quickly fishermen separate the good from the bad of the catch? They must work quickly to save the best, and they know at a glance what qualifies. Sometimes we question their throwaways, particularly if the discarded in question looks perfectly fine, but these fishermen have been at this awhile and really don't need our help. Neither does God.

If you're already familiar with the parable of the fishing nets, you know Jesus is talking about the Last Judgment. You know, the judgment where we are in the net?

Too often we think we are the fishermen or, at least, an assistant to them.

How many times have we forged a relationship with a non-Christian, opened ourselves up to questions about our beliefs—only to have our faith rejected? Or made fun of, particularly if a nonbeliever deems our responses unsatisfactory? "Well!" we huff. Or we cry over their lost soul. Or we abandon that person who didn't accept our invitation at the precise time we offered it, so now he or she is running behind schedule. Our schedule, that is.

Let's not lose sight of who we are in this parable: we are fish in the net. We don't do the catching, and we don't do the separating. What we can do, however, is obey the Great Commission and tell others about the Source of our joy. We cannot determine their response or the timing of their response. It may take two years, ten years, or twenty-five years for them to come to Christ—or they may never do so. This passage clearly indicates that some won't. But we can't possibly know another's heart the way God does—which is why Jesus has us all caught up in the same net.

Be strong enough not to let any sort of rejection of God's truth affect how you relate to nonbelievers. Whether they embrace what you're saying, put distance between the two of you, or sneer, reflect to them the Jesus you know and love. Just because we're all caught up in the same net doesn't mean we fall into the same trap.

Lord Jesus, help me seek and develop authentic relationships with those who do not know You, even if I am unaware of their spiritual status. Help me find the right "voice" when I represent You, whether I speak through my actions or my words. Prepare my heart and mind for any specific questions that may arise. Give me listening ears when nonbelievers speak. Let me hear as You hear.

BIG ROCKS AND
BIG PICTURES

*And the L*ORD *said, "Here is a place by Me, and you shall stand on the rock.*
So it shall be, while My glory passes by, that I will put you in the cleft of the rock,
and will cover you with My hand while I pass by. Then I will take away My hand,
and you shall see My back; but My face shall not be seen."

EXODUS 33: 21–23

Some beaches, and some points in beaches, are not lovely expanses of soft sand; rather, they have steep cliffs, sharp crags, and big, jagged rocks. The waves crash upon them, disintegrating back into the deep, only to return again. If you're seated high enough on such a rock, you won't be overcome, but you will feel the spray of the waves.

If you want to explore among these rocks you can expect a slow climb—and usually a steep and slippery ascent. The terrain is very unforgiving; you can bruise or bleed easily with one misstep. If you ever have an opportunity, visit a rocky portion of beach. Rub your hand along its surface; look upon its formation. And think about how Moses would climb this sort of terrain to communicate with God.

On this particular visit, Moses wanted assurance that God was there, not only in the immediate present, but would also be with him and the other leaders as they led the Hebrews out of Egypt. Moses wanted to experience God's glory.

Mind you, this was *after* the burning bush, after the plagues, after the mass exodus, after the parting of the Red Sea, after the golden calf incident. *How could Moses ask such a thing?* Was it not obvious God was with Him? We see a bigger picture, made up of various events that are clear indications that answer Moses' question; but Moses had to take his faith journey a day at a time. Moses saw evidence of God's *power*, but he wanted to see His *glory* as an assurance.

Think about how very similar Moses' prayers were to ours today. Do we ask for reassurance? How do we know God is with us? How has God shown us favor?

We can only know the answer to those questions by reflecting on what He has done in our lives—by stepping back and looking at the bigger picture. Like Moses, we can only see where God has passed by. That is the perspective He allows, and it reassures us that He was with us in the past, But He is also with us in the present, and He will be with us in the future. Thanks to His Son, we can experience God's mercy, compassion, forgiveness . . . and we can see His glory in a very personal way.

Father God, during those times I feel as though I'm climbing my own slippery, rocky slopes, I am reminded of Moses' request. I ask for peace as I reflect on the times I have experienced Your presence and knew You were there with me, so that I know You are still there with me and will continue to be there.

HERMIT CRABS

You know we never used flattery, nor did we put on a mask
to cover up greed—God is our witness.

1 THESSALONIANS 2:5 NIV

If you put a clean, empty seashell on a beach and it's spotted by a hermit crab, the crab will move in, and another will move into its abandoned shell. And so on. And so on. It's an interesting effect. All it takes is for one crab to make a move, and the others will follow. Do you have friends like that? Or enemies—or "frienemies," if you will? Is there someone who imitates your every move, but may or may not be very nice to you?

Maybe you bought a particular pair of shoes or got a new haircut, and this person copied your style. Perhaps you were recognized at work for solving a problem, only to have your supervisor accuse you of trying to take his or her job. Or perhaps you know someone whose supposed compliment is worded or delivered in such a way that you know you're being mocked. Regardless of that person's motives, the situation can be frustrating.

Flattery is a tough number, but when it's coupled with envy, we need to be on our guard—whether it's directed toward us, or we're directing it toward others. Let's look at David and Paul, two great examples of how these situations should be handled.

Paul was accused of flattering his audience and altering his message to believers in Thessalonica. It's true, Paul looked for common ground with those he was trying to reach, but he was not in this for the money and fame. Truly, he could have remained Saul and advanced his self-interests much, much easier. As Paul ministered, he did not seek people's admiration, nor did he seek to burden them under the fact of his being a man of God (vv. 6–8).

David handled King Saul's flattery and envy with great care. He remained humble and continued to serve God by serving Saul with integrity. God had promised David the throne, and David could have hastened his claim on occasion. But David wisely waited for God and honorably served a king who actually feared and despised him (1 Samuel 18).

Paul and David lived in very different circumstances, but they gave little attention to gushing. Knowing that they could not read minds nor hearts, neither man believed his own hype—Paul was sincere in his message; David took compliments in stride—and both trusted God with the rest.

As difficult as it may be for you to imagine, there are people out there who want what you have: your wardrobe, your husband, your lifestyle, even your faith. Sometimes, they are motivated because they want to *be like* you; other times it's because they secretly wish they *were* you. Like the examples of David and Paul, we need to keep pointing them toward the One *we're* trying to be like and disregard the rest.

Father, keep my heart and motives pure, whether I am the object of flattery or I want to compliment others. You give me value—and no one else can add to it nor diminish it.

MYSTERIES

These people draw near to Me with their mouth,

And honor Me with their lips,

But their heart is far from Me.

And in vain they worship Me,

Teaching as doctrines the commandments of men.

MATTHEW 15:8–9

Many beaches have some sort of ghost story or mystery attached to them. South Carolina's Grand Strand has the Gray Man and Alice Flagg. Various ghosts (including that of the father of Alexander Graham Bell) are rumored to roam Melville Bell Colonial Beach in Virginia. And if you're anywhere near a coast, locals and fishermen always have a strange story or occurrence that's part of the beach's folklore.

Too often we view God the same way. And our commitment to Him shows it. We love hearing tall tales that can do nothing more than give us goosebumps; yet, we yawn at the beautiful mysteries and miracles of God—accounts that reveal His character and set forth truth and promises for each one of us.

We sit in our pews each Sunday, bored. We're there for our kids, really. It is, after all, the thing to do. Going to church is what makes us "good people." *When is lunch? What time does the game start? How late is that store open?*

How real is God to you? We like to mention God in very trite, but dramatic ways—"Well, of course you need God" or "God is watching over us"—but whose god are you talking about? Do you treat Him as though He is real?

Do you take time to engage Him? Devote time to meditate on His truths—or are you too busy cycling through your to-do list for the day? When a blessing arrives, do you take time to stop and sincerely thank the One who provided it—or do you consider it merely a stroke of luck and say a quick, "ThankyouJesus"?

When you choose one of the last two options, our God diminishes into folklore—a warm presence we like to have around, but certainly not enough for Him to permeate our lives.

We need God. He is watching over us, but He is not a legend or a nice story or even a scary story! He is our Creator who knows us intimately and wants us to know Him in the same way.

When we relegate God to a checklist or empty words, we are mocking Him much like the soldiers who gave Jesus the crown of thorns (Matthew 27:29).

God is not the protagonist in a charming old tale peppered with a few little life lessons that children should know. Nor is He "up there," waiting to zap us with a stun gun if we don't go through the proper religious motions. Our God is alive. He is powerful, and He wants us to feel His very powerful, very real presence.

Lord, so many, many directions and distractions call to me. My heart is empty, my commitment to You is stale. I need to focus. Help me shut out all extraneous thoughts and let me feel Your presence, hear Your voice, taste Your goodness. Let me feel Your grace and mercy wash over my repentant heart.

MANATEES

LORD, all my desire is before You;
And my sighing is not hidden from You. . . .
My loved ones and my friends stand aloof . . .
And my relatives stand afar off.

PSALM 38:9, 44

Manatees are plant-eating mammals with no known enemies. Their survival skills are quite impressive, and their gray-to-white brain matter proportion is even greater than humans. In recent years, they've garnered a lot of attention, primarily because they are an endangered species. Yet, they are solitary creatures.

While many single women may identify with the manatee, it is not their choice nor desire to be alone. And to add insult to injury, they may be shunned or ignored by friends, family, and, yes, even churches—ranging anywhere from social invitations, not fitting into a church's programming, or even being relegated to the kids' table at holidays, because, you know . . . "you're single."

Women get married for myriad reasons, and not always for love. And it's true that marriage doesn't solve problems; it can, in fact, create more (1 Corinthians 7:28). And of married women, plenty are lonely.

But these factors still do not resolve the yearning for those who want to be married.

Whether our desires haven't aligned with God's, or marriage is not in His timing yet (or at all), these feelings are very real and the void is very present—and therefore should not be discounted by anyone. You *are* whole. No other person can contribute to or take away from the completeness of God in you, so don't give credence to those who try.

To ask that God take hold of our sense and sensibilities on this issue is a step in the right direction. Taking responsibility for our attitude and behavior, of course, is another.

So ask God to plant women in your life who can be a source of encouragement as you figure out this journey He has you traveling. Do you know anyone whom you consider a spiritual mentor? Someone who, married or single, lives a life that demonstrates wisdom and peace? Spend time developing those relationships to help bring balance to your life.

You may be single, but you're not alone. And none of us are meant to live like the manatee. Whether you're unmarried for a season or for a lifetime, relish the freedom and fullness that singleness offers, including the opportunity to choose for yourself a family of encouragers and supporters.

Lord, I have a special desire to meet someone with whom I can share this journey. I would love that someone to be my husband, one chosen by You, especially for me, if it is in Your will. In the meantime, help me find those who will encourage me to discover Your specific will for me, so that my desires align fully with Yours.

BARNACLES

Since we are surrounded by so great a cloud of witnesses,
let us lay aside every weight, and the sin which so easily ensnares us,
and let us run with endurance the race that is set before us.

HEBREWS 12:1

Barnacles live in fairly shallow water, attaching themselves to hard surfaces and staying put. You'll see them accumulate on just about anything that doesn't move or isn't properly maintained.

Once they've established themselves, the only way to be rid of them is to blast them off with a high-pressure sprayer or scrape them off with a special tool. Interestingly enough, these creatures grow thicker in fast-moving water, such as when they're attached to the hull of a moving boat.

When barnacles accumulate on the hull of a sailboat, they can interfere with its propellers and noticeably hinder its speed. Likewise, our thoughts and actions, even our health, can be hindered when we are weighed down by sin.

We are required to slough off—or, since we're women, *exfoliate*—anything weighing us down or hindering us from an optimum spiritual journey. As in the case of barnacles, these hindrances do not go away by themselves. They accumulate, they build, they fester. A small argument left unresolved, a vice that we cannot shake, a hurt we cannot release, an unforgiving attitude. And as we grow spiritually, so do the barnacles—just as they do in fast-moving water. So this task is perpetual.

Paul didn't give us an option here. He didn't say, "Try to get rid of most of your sins. If a few hang on, just plod on through." Nope, Paul was clear: every bit of our sin must go. Any one of them will slow us down, affect our witness, affect ourselves. Blasting or scraping off may be painful, but healing comes quicker, and strength will follow.

What will you exfoliate today?

Lord, I need to release _____ into Your hands right now. Please show me other barnacles on my spirit, that I may rid myself of them, as well.

THE PATH LESS TAKEN

Now an angel of the Lord spoke to Philip, saying,
"Arise and go toward the south along the road which goes down
from Jerusalem to Gaza." This is desert.

ACTS 8:26

I f you visit friends who live on the coast, they will know of a local path to the beach. You may walk over wooden planks instead of pristine boardwalks, and the occasional thorn may stick you, but once you've arrived, chances are good you're at a prime beach location. It's the spot barely dotted with tight-lipped locals who quietly allow rows and rows of tourists to pack in from an entry point at a much farther distance.

Crowds were packing in to hear Philip preach and see him perform miracles. He had no plans to leave Samaria, and eventually Peter and John were sent there as well. Then, just like that, God sent word to Philip that he must hit the desert road—and he had no idea why.

How many of us would have said, "But have you seen the crowds who are coming to worship? Why am I being sent to the desert alone?"

In Philip's case, we know the answer to that last question: God wanted Peter to encounter the Ethiopian official. Then, immediately following, Philip vanished into thin air—but this brief encounter ultimately delivered the gospel to Ethiopia.

Following Christ involves taking a less populated and, often lesser-known, path. Sometimes this path is not well-defined, so you find that your steps are more hopeful than sure. Pardon the pun, but it can often feel like a path that's "beneath" you.

Philip was drawing crowds, but was suddenly sent to the desert to talk to a single man. How many of us would walk away from the adoration and admiration of the masses to travel to a desolate place for one conversation? God didn't send Philip to the desert forever—just for a moment. And what a moment it was!

The path less taken does have its advantages. It gives you an opportunity to view God's creation as He intended it—wild and free, not safe and manicured. Without all the noise, you hear His voice more easily. You're not fighting crowds who have chosen an easier, more obvious route. No, this less-traveled path gives you quiet solitude, populated only by those who reside there or who have walked this same path previously.

And you learn that, if you must, you can travel this path alone. Because if you know who is leading you, you know where it leads.

Lord, I may choose a different path to the beach today as a reminder that Your path is different from all that the world offers. Yours is the only path to eternal life.

LEAFY SEA DRAGONS

*"What do you benefit if you gain the whole world
but lose your own soul?"*

MARK 8:36 NLT

Leafy sea dragons—or "leafies"—look like seahorses that have sprouted seaweed, an appearance that protects them from would-be predators. Depending on the dragon's age, diet, and stress levels, some of these creatures can also change color to further camouflage themselves. (On a side note, these critters lay bright pink eggs!)

The sea dragon's entire life is spent fitting in, blending in, even wearing a disguise. And this basic approach to life is its means for survival. Too often, we think the same is true for us—that we need to focus on fitting in, blending in with the crowd, even wearing a disguise.

Why do we spend so much time and effort trying to please a particular crowd? The cool group at our high school, the best sorority in college, the mover-shaker crowd and society mavens in our communities, or even, yes, the inner circle at church. Whoever it is at this stage of life, we scheme about how to be in their presence. We study their habits and strategize how to make them accept us—and it's hard work, trying to be something we're not.

Sometimes our disguises succeed, but our time of fitting in will be short-lived if the group's values and activities run counter to our Christian faith. Eventually, we will have to decide: do we add more camouflage, or do we reveal our real identity as a child of God?

It's a risk, being the you God created and intends you to be. But genuine peace comes only when we live out our faith as authentically as possible. As the psalmist declared, "I would rather be a doorkeeper in the house of my God than dwell in the tents of wickedness" (Psalm 84:10 NIV).

So the next time you're at the beach, purchase something small and bright pink—a colored shell, a polished rock, a change purse, even a cheapie ring with a bright pink stone. Keep it as a reminder of the leafy's egg and what the leafy has to do to survive. We, on the other hand, have a choice.

Father, I want to take a moment to consider the relationships You want for me versus the ones I chase after. Reveal to me those people who belong to You, individuals who will encourage me and edify me. Let me pursue friendship with them. Give me the courage to show my true colors—the characteristics, traits, passions, and idiosyncrasies You painted me with.

Rescue by Vomit

And [Jonah] said: "I cried out to the LORD because of my affliction,
And He answered me.
Out of the belly of Sheol I cried,
And You heard my voice. . . ."
So the Lord spoke to the fish, and it vomited Jonah onto dry land.

Jonah 2:2, 10

When the lifeguard's whistle blows, an ambulance arrives out of nowhere, beach patrol shouts through a bullhorn, and leisurely tourists become upright onlookers—something has happened. Someone got caught in the riptide and the situation is life or death. Fatigued, the swimmer does not have the ability to swim back to shore. Someone must rescue him.

This was Jonah's predicament. He'd been running from God and realized he couldn't escape on his own. There he was, in the belly of a fish, certain that this was the end. He could not save himself, for there was no way out. So—and feel free to chuckle here—Jonah was rescued by way of vomit.

Many times the Lord walks through the fires and waves with us, but there are times He simply plucks us out of a situation—perhaps one we are either unwilling or unable to leave ourselves—and rescues us.

And, like Jonah's rescue (again, feel free to chuckle), it's not always the most obvious form of rescue. Sometimes our hearts are broken in the process. Sometimes we are asked to leave a job we love—or even a job we don't, but desperately need. Sometimes we must leave behind all that we've ever known. And the longer we cling to what we know—the unknown is so scary, after all—the more painful and more difficult the rescue efforts become. Would you be as stubborn if you were drowning or trapped? Taking a cue from Jonah's story, we might need to be vomited out of a situation right now. There will be time for questions later.

During these doesn't-seem-like-a-rescue events in our lives, we may get angry. We may cry. We may bargain with God, but this is not a street market. We may beg God for a different outcome—change the person, have the employer admit the mistake and rehire you—whatever it is. We can ask, and God certainly has the power to do whatever He wishes. But His ways are not ours. His perspective transcends anything we could possibly realize this side of heaven. Our vantage point is very limited, and we can't see into the future.

We can ask God to show us why He's doing what He's doing, and one day He might. But more importantly is the day that we can say with a full heart, "No, I don't see. But I trust."

Lord, I have been thinking about _____
and how suddenly that situation turned. I don't understand. I was so much happier back then. But I know in my heart I did all I could do, and Your answer is that it's done. Help me grow in my trust that You have rescued me from something I may never have to know about or understand.

SUNSET

*"I do not pray for these alone, but also for
those who will believe in Me through their word."*

JOHN 17:20

Today, watch the sunset in all its majesty and . . . remember.

Long ago—nearly two thousand years, actually—the sun was setting. But Jesus' work was not done.

So much He needed to say—and He had to move quickly. But as He taught His brothers, evening settled in and He was not finished. There was Another with whom He needed to speak.

As Jesus wandered to the garden that night to pray over a multitude of things, He knew what He was facing; yet, most of His prayer was devoted to those believers who would follow—in the coming days, in the coming years, and in the coming centuries.

Here was a Man facing death, whose main concern was for those who'd never dined with Him, walked with Him, or traveled with Him. They had not been there when He taught from the boat. Or on the mountain. Or in the temple courts. But that didn't matter; they would follow in due time.

That night, Jesus prayed for you. A short time later, His work would be complete. For us all.

What sorts of things do we do in a day? Laundry. Homework. Grocery shopping. The bills get paid, doctor and dentist appointments are made. We finish a big project for work or school, or we plant a garden. We clean our homes. We eat our meals. And yes, we even plan our Sunday school lessons.

But in the process of doing our tasks, do we miss something? Do we miss Jesus in the activities of our day? Do we miss the One who did not let His day, nor His life, end without praying for us?

The sun did not set on that day without Jesus taking time to make His petition to His Father. The One who had the power to stop the sun from setting altogether elected instead to complete the prophecy and redeem us all.

As you watch tonight's sunset, think about that sunset two thousand years ago. What have you left undone today?

Lord, I watch the sun set on the horizon and think about what I accomplished and what I have left undone. I confess that some days, I am so focused on getting daily tasks complete, I forget to spend time with the Redeemer who completed me. Out of gratitude and love I come to You now. Give me patience to leave some things undone, that I may spend more time with You.

STAGNANT AIR

Men will stagger from sea to sea
and wander from north to east,
*searching for the word of the L*ORD,
but they will not find it.
"In that day,
the lovely young women and
strong young men
will faint because of thirst."

AMOS 8:12–13 NIV

There are days when relief just won't come. You've anticipated that the day would be a hot one, but not like this. The sun is boiling, there is no breeze, the umbrella isn't helping, your head is sopping wet from the sun hat, and you're fanning yourself with a magazine, bound and determined to stay put. You're running through water bottles like there's no tomorrow. And for someone out there, there isn't one.

Many studies agree that by the time you realize you're thirsty, you're already dehydrated. This is also true for thirsty souls. Amos was in a tight spot. The Israelites had been thrilled when this ordinary layman and unlikely prophet delivered a message of death and destruction for all the nations they despised. But eventually, the same message was delivered *to* them, *about* them. Well, for Amaziah the priest, Amos had gone too far. Now he was just causing trouble, and he needed to go back to his sheep. Enough was enough. And it would have been so easy for Amos to do so—except for his faithful, obedient heart.

At this point, the Israelites were searching anywhere and everywhere for answers to their problems while overlooking the needs of others. God and His commands were more of a nuisance, really. Amos warned the people of Israel that they were headed for a time when they would earnestly search for a word from God and not be quenched. God's life-giving truth would, from their perspective, be taken away.

God's warnings are often uncomfortable to study and absorb because they do not appear to be borne out of love. They indicate His frustration, His anger, even His hatred. It's too easy to look at the behavior of the ancient Israelites and *judge* instead of *relate*. So before we judge how silly they were, let's step back for a second: Have we not looked for relief everywhere except the Lord? We poll friends, lose our identities in our families, chase status, cling to possessions, put our bodies through untold abuse, want church to be over because a cute guy asked us to lunch, compare our wardrobes and relationships to those on a favorite television program or magazine, criticize or make fun of another person to show how smart we are . . . because at some point, human admiration makes us valuable. Or at least makes everyone think we are. Which means, truly, no relief for our spirits.

We, too, are parched. We are thirsty. And we have been warned.

Lord Jesus, I confess that I turn too often to opinions and things that are temporary when Your promise is eternal. I look for answers and fulfillment in other people, other things, thinking that another human being or an inanimate object will give me value and status. I confess that I elevate them and give them power that rightfully belongs to You. Turn my head and my heart, Lord.

LIGHTHOUSES

Do not gloat over me, my enemy!
Though I have fallen, I will rise.
Though I sit in darkness,
the LORD will be my light.

MICAH 7:8 NIV

They are mysterious, solitary, and majestic. No two are the same, but they serve a common purpose: to identify treacherous terrain and cut through fog and darkness, enabling safe passage for those who will heed their warning.

Our Lord desires to be the same sort of beacon in our lives, but sometimes that can leave us feeling lonely or impatient. Or both.

The prophet Micah felt very alone too. God sent him to not only identify the injustices and infections of worldly interests occurring in Israel and Judah, but also to warn them about the possible consequences of inauthentic faith. As you can imagine, this message didn't make Micah a popular guy.

In fact, Micah probably looked ridiculous. Here was this poor guy, ranting about waiting on God and telling them their religion is polluted. But their religion came from God, right? Their rituals and practices were God-instructed—with a few more things thrown in, of course, to keep up with the times and, you know, to get the government off their backs. And the priests were dressed appropriately, Israel was getting rich and fat—this must mean that God was okay with what they were doing. So why listen to the crazy guy spouting stuff about humility and repentance? Get with the program, Micah! All seems to be working just fine!

But just like the view from the top of a lighthouse, the perspective is very different and much broader than that from the beach or the sea. God's omniscient perspective was very different from Israel's, yet Israel was too proud to heed His warning because they were focused on enjoying comfort and prosperity.

In worldly terms, the book of Micah ends as a cliffhanger. We know what happened to Israel, but we don't know what happened to Micah. We do know that he was willing to sit in the dark, alone, and wait on God. How long did he wait? Did he have moments of despair as he waited patiently for God's beacon? We certainly do. We feel as though we are drifting, going nowhere, because we hear nothing from God.

The temptation to strike out on our own is strong, but consider the ship that disregards a lighthouse: the ship will make progress and may even succeed for a while, but ultimately, it hastens its own destruction. It's an especially foolish plan when the captain knows better. Metaphorically speaking, this is what happened to Israel who thought she knew better.

In times of uncertainty and definitive destruction, wait on God. Even when you don't want to.

Lord, forgive my impatience—but where are You? Open my ears if I am not listening, open my eyes if I'm not seeing, and open my heart so that I may learn the joy of waiting on You. Give me Your strength that I may resist the temptation to resolve this matter with my own methods. Send me Your light as my trust in Your timing grows!

WATER, WATER EVERYWHERE

Jesus answered and said to [the Samaritan woman at the well],
"If you knew the gift of God, and who it is who says to you,
'Give Me a drink,' you would have asked Him,
and He would have given you living water."

JOHN 4:10

It's interesting that while we're surrounded by water at the beach, it's not drinkable. It's beautiful, it's soothing, it's refreshing to splash in, but it will not give our bodies any of the necessary fluid we must have each day.

People are fearfully and wonderfully made by God—and, physically, we require water each day. So it's no wonder that our spirits—that part of us that will live on beyond the physical—require "living water" in order to do so. And it's no wonder why many of us remain parched. And why, sadly, many of us die inside.

Since the dawn of time, not one person on the planet has received life without God. He is our common denominator. It makes sense, then, that He would be our authentic Source for living water. Yet, too often, we look for other sources.

Even believers tend to forget how much they need living water. Just like the ocean water, we surround ourselves with symbols, texts, music, jewelry, art—"God stuff," if you will—and we lose sight of God Himself. We'd rather splash around in the supplemental than quench our thirsts with the fresh flow of living water.

Supplemental materials or symbolic pieces serve as an extension or expression—and can be very helpful for reinforcing our faith—but they are by no means a substitute for direct, personal encounters with God Himself. They do not give life or replenish.

Jesus describes living water to a woman who thinks He means that, literally, she would not have need to return to the well each day, which certainly would have made life easier for her (John 4:15). But following Christ doesn't guarantee an easy life; rather, daily, hourly, constant replenishment of living water certainly gives us a perspective and strength to endure it . . . and even, usually, to authentically *enjoy* it.

Look around the beach today. Find the sweatiest person there—even if it's a complete stranger—and offer her a bottle of water from your stash. Watch the expression on her face, the gratitude that's there as she opens the bottle and drinks. Listen to her sighs of relief and observe her satisfied smile as her thirst is quenched. She will need water again at some point, but for the moment, she is filled with the very best thing to replenish herself.

Our spirits have the same opportunity—and we are free to drink as often as needed.

Lord, let me not forget that my strongest growth and biggest spiritual leaps come from encountering You each day. As I read the Scriptures, meditate on Your creation, or interact with others, let me receive Your living water and receive authentic refreshment.

CABANAS

Then Jael, Heber's wife, took a tent peg and took a hammer in her hand,
and went softly to [Sisera, the commander at the Canaanite army] and drove the peg into his temple,
and it went down into the ground; for he was fast asleep and weary. So he died.

JUDGES 4:21

There are some beaches left that still rent cabanas—those cute little makeshift tents used to store items, cool off, and change clothes, et cetera. They provide various forms of respite and privacy. The kind that Sisera, commander of King Jabin's army, was in search of when he fled the battlefield. It was unfortunate for him that he entered the tent of one independent-minded, courageous woman: Jael.

It's been suggested that Heber's was a family of tinsmiths and had moved their camp closer to the battlefield to supply Canaanite soldiers with weapons. (That would explain Jael's one expert blow to Sisera's head!) And because it was customary that a man take more than one wife, it was not unusual for Jael to have her own private tent.

By law, Heber and Jael were required to follow a strict code of hospitality that included protection and care for visitors. But only the head of the household could offer this particular sort of hospitality—certainly not his wife. Sisera made a wrong assumption to think that Jael would oblige or that she didn't know her politics.

Certainly Jael heard enough talk around the camp, and especially from her own husband, about the current climate between Israel and Canaan. It would have been easier and culturally acceptable for her to just go along with whatever she heard. But her loyalty remained with God of Israel, not her culture.

Consider the risks this woman took. She made up her own mind—and went against her husband's beliefs, values, and politics—because she knew right from wrong. She knew she was risking her own life, but obedience to God was more important. God was then able to use her quick mind and skillful hand to ultimately bring down the entire Canaanite nation, giving respite not only to herself, but all of Israel.

God gifted us all with brains unlike any other creature on earth. We are to use our minds and our abilities in ways that glorify and honor Him. When we allow others to form our opinions or tell us what we are to think, we may be handing God back His gift and saying, "No, thanks." Can another person know our place better than the One who created us?

Father, through the blood of Jesus, I have a direct line of communication with You; the curtain was torn at Calvary. While others try to influence me—friends, family members, media—remind me that You also gave me discernment to sift through and check the facts for myself. Thank You that I may also search out the truth by way of the Scriptures, prayer, and the truths You embed in my heart. Let me hear Your voice over all others.

SUNBURNS AND SUNBLOCK

For what credit is it if, when you are beaten for your faults,

you take it patiently? But when you do good and suffer,

if you take it patiently, this is commendable before God.

1 PETER 2:20

It's happened to all of us: we take great care to put on our sunblock, and we miss a spot. So we wind up with this weird, usually hand-shaped sunburn in a summertime-conspicuous place, like our décolletages, behind a calf, or—gulp—our faces. This is what we get for our efforts? So much for our even-toned tans!

The burned portion leaves a spot on us that's vulnerable and unprotected. It's painful and may require special care, like aloe or lotion. Sometimes, the pain our vulnerable parts endure is less conspicuous, but the attack is very real.

To varying extremes, we as believers will suffer for God. Many of us will never endure the kind of physical torture Peter did, but there are any number of people willing to punish us for no other reason than standing firm in our faith. This harassment could come in the form of mockery, trickery, or deception—and we're left feeling exposed, hurt, humiliated. The Enemy delights in messing with our minds to cause pain in our hearts.

Peter spoke about our hurts here, explaining that we are to be commended if we suffer for the wrong reasons; for "doing good." But look at the next part of his statement: *if . . . you take it patiently.*

Sometimes we just lose our cool. Other times we're confrontational or hotly defensive. Or we smugly tell those who intend to harm us that we'll "pray for them." We feel righteous, taking a hit for the Lord, don't we? We yell, we fight, we push back, and when the situation still doesn't go our way, we call it "persecution."

Friend, you may be suffering, but you are not being persecuted.

And when we respond in such a way, particularly with a nonbeliever, you are not representing our Christ. When you encounter opposition or prejudice against Christ—yes, those *intent on making you suffer*—consider this person's spirit. They were created by God just as you were, but perhaps their past is filled with poor representations of Christ. They don't know Him because they have "religion" confused with faith. Christ said not everyone will enter the kingdom of heaven (Matthew 7:21), but that's not our concern; making disciples is. Or should be (Matthew 28:19). When we attack back in response, why would anyone think Jesus offers a better, life-changing way of life?

To paraphrase Christ, nonbelievers *know not what they do.* Each day, bathe yourself in God's protection. Slather it on good and thick. But if you miss a spot and get burned, treat it patiently. As Romans 14:1 says, "Accept him whose faith is weak, without passing judgment on disputable matters" (NIV).

Lord, when I suffer on Your behalf, grant me godly patience as others search for my most vulnerable spots to burn. Cover me in the kind of patience that even surprises me, and I'll know it's from You. Then when I do respond, I will—by Your grace—respond as You would.

OFF DUTY

There is no healing for your wound;
your injury is fatal.
All who hear of your destruction
will clap their hands for joy.
Where can anyone be found
who has not suffered from your continual cruelty?

NAHUM 3:19 NLT

There's something a bit unnerving about an empty lifeguard chair, isn't there? It seems abandoned, and for a brief moment, we may feel that we are too.

It's no wonder that beach lifeguards must undergo a considerable amount of training. They have a lot of responsibilities that extend beyond supervising a defined stretch of beach: first aid, EMS, and rescue. They use various tools to communicate—whistles, megaphones, bullhorns—and make every effort to keep the environment safe and enjoyable. While they hold a very powerful position, it's one exclusively of service.

Sometimes we attempt to be a lifeguard of our friends. We want to call out to those who stray, save the ones who are out too far, and make every effort to keep them safe from harm. It's a noble quest, and we should be willing to reach out and help our friends. But without proper boundaries, we can easily become someone's personal lifeguard.

Before you start distancing yourself from various people in your life, ask yourself some tough questions. Why is this person important to you? Do you truly feel called to help them? Do you have an intimate understanding of the situation, or are you trying to replace the role of a professional? If they are fighting an addiction, for example? Do you—deep down—want to be the one who "saved" this person? The one who never gave up on them?

Certainly, we give special consideration to those who are trying, even when they stumble. *Especially* if they stumble. And depending on the situation, they may be facing a lot of rejection and peer judgment. But prayerful consideration must be given when we're getting emotionally and physically drained by someone, or even wanting glory and power for "saving" them. Sometimes the best way to offer a person support is to take a few steps back. Not to turn on them, not to turn away from them, but to find an alternate way to support them without losing yourself in the process. If we ourselves do not have a clear understanding of healthy boundaries among friends, we risk enabling instead of helping, controlling instead of encouraging. In our attempt to love, we become a stumbling block to their healing.

We simply cannot be all things to all people. We are not trained to do this, nor is it possible. It's time to leave the lifeguard's chair; that role belongs to Another.

Lord, today I will commit to going off duty and no longer sit in the lifeguard's chair. Help me set healthy boundaries and identify those who are toxic. Make me sensitive and aware of those I can help, even if just for a season, and enable me to gently release the others into Your care.

SHARK'S TEETH

We were therefore buried with him through baptism into death
in order that, just as Christ was raised from the dead through the glory
of the Father, we too may live a new life.

ROMANS 6:4 NIV

Have you ever been lucky enough to find a shark's tooth while strolling on the beach? Maybe you were wandering along the tide lines at low tide, or you ventured out to a nearby sandbar. That's usually where you'll find these triangular-shaped teeth, ranging anywhere from tiny to nearly six inches in length.

If you find one, however, keep in mind that you've probably found a fossil. It often takes years for a shark's tooth to settle in sediment on the ocean floor, fossilize, and re-emerge by washing up on the beach. Depending on the type of minerals and sediment in which they've settled, shark's teeth fossilize into different colors as the sediment replaces the actual tooth. By the time the now-fossilized tooth re-emerges, it's possible that it is centuries upon centuries old—possibly having belonged to a species long extinct.

Thank goodness our salvation doesn't require that much time to work out, yet we can learn a lot from parallels between the processes.

Like a shark's lost tooth, our souls are lost. We drift and sink at the same time, until we reach the floor of our despair. Everyone's "sediment" is different and, therefore, will affect us differently. For believers, how wonderful it is that the Holy Spirit fills our hearts and replaces our sinful natures immediately. As humans, however, we know that growing holy is a lifelong process. Nonetheless, a new creature emerges: our former lives and purposes are now extinct. And though our transformation takes our entire lives, it will be done (Philippians 4:6).

Lord, thank You for assuring my future as a new creature by way of Your Son. Thank You for the hope that sustains me each day, a hope that will be fully realized in eternity.

HURRICANES

And the LORD said to Moses, "Why do you cry to Me?
Tell the children of Israel to go forward."

EXODUS 14:15

W hen a hurricane is forecast, many precautions are taken: sandbags are gathered, disaster kits are put together, boats are secured, evacuations are planned, and so on. Believers and nonbelievers alike take steps to avoid disaster and keep people and pets safe. It just makes good sense.

So why, when disaster strikes at home, do we shrug and say, "All I can do is pray"? Short answer: No, it's not.

There they were, the Israelites, whining to Moses about how they should have remained in Egpyt. They could see Pharoah and his army approaching, and things did not look good. Moses told them that they needed only to be still—but God had a different response.

Yes, we are to spend time in prayer for daily guidance, long-term guidance, and communion. We praise, we confess, we petition, we ask questions, we cry . . . prayer is our primary way of connecting to Him. And there are times, as Moses directed, when we need to be still and wait for Him. As believers, praying is part of what we do. But as the Lord stated here, it's not *all* we can do.

Too often, prayer is an excuse for delayed reaction or not doing anything at all. We justify our inaction by saying that God is all-knowing and all-powerful, so if we pray about it, somehow He will spring to action.

And yes, it's true that God does not *need* us to carry out His plan, but at times He *wants* us involved. He wants us to get our hands dirty, because quite often He reveals Himself in these situations. When you look at the problems and epidemics that plague our communities, disasters that strike other nations, famine, abuse, adultery, homelessness, addiction, and other heartbreaking situations all around us—even in our own families—it's apparent that there are plenty of directions we can go in.

If a friend is making a wrong decision, a community is in turmoil, or a disruptive stranger is on the street, God may be impressing more than prayer on your heart. He may be summoning you to take action. If that's the case, trust that He will equip you—or change your direction, if necessary. You may not be parting the Red Sea, as Moses did, but be assured you are making an impact for the kingdom.

Father God, let me not forget in my petitions that I ask You what action, if any, I am to take—and let me do so without fear and reservation. And Lord, if I take a step in the wrong direction, I trust and pray that You will make my path straight.

PEBBLE BEACHES

A man's steps are directed by the LORD.
How then can anyone understand their own way?

PROVERBS 20:24 NIV

Pebble beaches are a bit of an enigma. Instead of soft sand, these beaches are primarily made up of little stones and other types of coarse material.

On a first visit, the term pebble beach can be misleading; they're *rocks*, for crying out loud. This isn't like the warm, soft, sandy beaches we're used to—the kind of sand that envelopes our feet. So how do we navigate our steps?

It isn't until our bare feet actually touch them that we realize the anticipation was worse than the actual experience. The stones are smooth and can be quite slippery. Perhaps we don't move as swiftly as we do on hard sand, perhaps it's not as squishy as dry sand, but we can definitely walk on this type of surface—even with bare feet. It's not nearly as painful as we thought. In some cases, it's not painful at all.

We anticipate certain events in our lives the same way. We dread performance reviews, report cards, medical test results; we delay difficult conversations with loved ones; we set ourselves up to be defensive with customer service. The list goes on. We get hyped up about situations and conversations, just knowing they're going to be awful. *Especially if we're the one who has messed up.*

This kind of thought process is defeating. We assume that we already know the outcome, as though we can read minds and predict the future. We can prepare for certain conditions and should. If God knows our steps, however, then we also need to trust Him with our path. We may even realize how much time we've wasted building up this situation in our heads instead of praying for wisdom and words.

So much can be defused by sincerely saying, "I messed up, and I'm sorry. Is there something I can do to help at this point?"

Before building a crisis in your head, stop the rush of thoughts, and pray. Pray for peace, pray for wisdom, and pray for words. Ask God to calm your anxiety and guide you.

And even if you don't completely understand what's going on, there is a point when you simply have to take off your shoes and walk through it—with Him. It's the only way to get to the next destination.

Father, when I am approaching tricky life terrain, I spend a lot of time in worry and anticipation. Then I build up my defenses when I don't even need them. When I encounter adversity, let me draw upon Your wisdom so I will know how to face the situation. And grant me the assurance that, no matter what the outcome, You are with me.

TURTLE WALKS

But He answered them, saying, "Who is My mother, or My brothers?"
and He looked around in a circle at those who sat about Him,
and said, "Here are My mother and My brothers!
For whoever does the will of God is My brother and My sister and mother."

MARK 3:33-35

If you're headed to the beach, see if a turtle walk will be happening during your stay. Whether or not one is scheduled will depend on your destination since the seasons differ. The season and destination will also determine whether you'll witness turtles nesting or hatching. (They do not nest on the West Coast.)

Once the females lay their eggs, they return to the water. The eggs are left alone together—and eventually they will hatch together. From there, they slowly plod together into the sea. Some walks, like those in Edisto Beach in South Carolina, allow participants to carry the baby hatchlings to the water to protect them from predators.

This natural kind of togetherness is an interesting observation, particularly if you grew up in a dysfunctional family or are estranged from your family of origin. Whether you were emotionally or physically abandoned, either you were left alone to sort out things that were confusing or you accepted your situation as normal—until, by the grace of God, you learned otherwise.

Healing begins and ends at the Cross. As today's scripture indicates, believers are members of a spiritual, eternal family who—when living in accordance with God's will—can provide healthy support and encouragement that some families of origin lack.

Just like the baby turtles, those in your community will sit with you and walk with you—and the Holy Spirit will carry you.

Father, it's upsetting when friends talk about shopping trips with their mothers or deep conversations with their fathers. I didn't have that; I still don't have that. Help me find my community, and help me reach out to others who are in the same situation I'm in. Together, we can discover the kind of nurturing and healing that You want for us.

SAND WAVES

Let us pursue the things which make for peace and
the things by which one may edify another.

ROMANS 14:19

You've seen them, those tight ripples on the sand, close to the water. These sand waves—or sand ridges—are formed by very strong currents or wind. Recent studies have indicated that fields of them lurk under water and continue building to a height that sometimes presents challenges to ships trying to navigate through them. Vessels with little under-keel clearance are at particular risk. Mariners must keep watch because even the latest surveys of a given field do not always reflect a sand wave's full height.

Unresolved conflict can have the same impact on us that sand waves can have on a boat. When hurt, pain, and sin remain unresolved, they continue to build. Ultimately, their presence can be treacherous as we navigate through life because, at some point, the buildup will affect us.

Maybe you broke someone's confidence; maybe someone broke yours. Maybe you have an addiction problem or have suffered because of someone else's addiction. Perhaps a terrible sin in your past—a sin someone committed against you or maybe one you yourself committed—has left you confused, isolated, distrusting. In situations like these, we too often skip over the healing process, scrambling to claim a false grace without really working through the pain with the Lord. We keep going in life without allowing Him to tear down the buildup and take away the toxic emotions and memories.

Just like sand waves, our pain or our lack of forgiveness can impact other aspects of our lives. Yet, we leave God out of this process of healing and forgiveness when we think He may insist we take a closer look at what happened. Doing so may force us to identify dangerous patterns—like those sand waves—and our own contributions to the situation. Or we might find ourselves reliving in our minds and hearts a certain experience that we'd rather bury even deeper.

That's what happens when we follow the Lord: His life-giving revelations of truth are certain, but the path of living in their light isn't always smooth. Making excuses is much easier, isn't it?

But we only hurt ourselves when we choose that option. God's desire is for us to open our minds and hearts and let Him help us tear down built-up sand waves and sweep away their pattern once and for all. Then, by His Spirit, He will show us what to watch for, should those patterns ever try to reestablish their presence in our lives.

Lord, reveal the sand waves in my life and what action, if any, I should take to remove them. You know better than I the experiences, hurts, and sin that threaten to build up to a dangerous height in my life. Give me courage to face what I need to face, to feel what I need to feel, and to forgive what I need to forgive, so that I can live in the freedom You long for me to know.

BEACH PLAY:
DOGS, CHILDREN, CELEBRATING

And Nehemiah, who was the governor, Ezra the priest and scribe, and the Levites who taught
the people said to all the people, "This day is holy to the LORD your God; do not mourn nor weep."
For all the people wept, when they heard the words of the Law. Then he said to them,
"Go your way, eat the fat, drink the sweet, and send portions to those for whom nothing is prepared;
for this day is holy to our LORD. Do not sorrow, for the joy of the LORD is your strength." . . .
And all the people went their way to eat and drink, to send portions and rejoice greatly,
because they understood the words that were declared to them.

NEHEMIAH 8:9–12

Have you ever watched dogs and children at play on the beach? They are un-leashed, unhindered, and ready to drink in all that the expanse has to offer. They run, jump, play, more raucous than usual—not to draw attention to them-selves, but rather out of the zeal felt toward their surroundings.

The Israelites were mournful and sad, having squarely faced God's law and how far they'd strayed from it. As they were humbled, like so many of us today, they de-veloped a woe-is-me attitude, intent on carrying around their guilt and shame. Some of them would lumber around in sackcloths, if they had any.

Yes, they were guilty. Yes, they should be ashamed and feel remorse. Those are key steps before genuine repentance. You see, humility is not about putting our-selves down. Humility involves recognizing our need for the Savior and what He has done for us. Now *that's* reason to celebrate!

And celebrate they did! They ate, they drank, and they shared their possessions so that no one—not even the poor—were excluded. They were humbled and grateful, thus honoring the Lord in their celebrations.

Solomon mentioned there being "a time for every purpose" (Ecclesiastes 3:4), and there are certainly times we will mourn. But consider the instructions Nehemiah and Ezra issued, and look at how children and dogs romp, fully enjoying God's creation in their play. God wants you to experience His goodness *now*, not just later!

And since there's no time like the present . . .

Lord, I am both humbled and awed that the Creator of everything knows me so intimately and loves me enough to give me eternal life, despite my shortcomings and sin. Thank You that I do not have to wait to experience Your goodness now and, thanks to Your Son, Jesus, I will one day celebrate it fully!

RUNNING ON THE BEACH

Everyone who competes in the games goes into strict training.
They do it to get a crown that will not last;
but we do it to get a crown that will last forever. Therefore I do not run like
a man running aimlessly; I do not fight like a man beating the air.

4 CORINTHIANS 9:25–26 NIV

Ask any runner—the most challenging terrain to run on is the beach. Some run barefoot while others wear shoes, but those who appear to do either effortlessly have been at it awhile. They have had to train and build up strength to make it look so easy.

Running on a softer surface requires better balance and more energy from the muscles involved. And for those who run barefoot, the sand allows the foot muscles to experience their natural range of motion.

Now there are plenty of risks, too—risks like sprains, strains, and puncture wounds, to name a few. And for a while, runners have to slow their pace, making them appear slower than they really are. So why do it?

Well, the payoff is worth it. These runners improve their strength and speed, they experience less impact, and they burn up to 4.6 times more calories per mile. Training on a beach can literally put more spring in their step when they run on a hard surface like asphalt. Otherwise, they are putting themselves through a lot of pain for no reason.

As you live out your faith, and run your own race, do you have days when you wonder what's the point? Admit it. At times, running the race God sets for each of us seems more difficult than giving in to sin or living mediocre, milquetoast lives.

Aren't there times when it would be easier to just go along with the herd? Or to simply be a spectator?

If these races of faith were always easy, everyone would be doing it and sticking with it.

There are risks involved when we accept and follow Jesus. Some of us even have to sacrifice favorite pastimes or possessions as part of our training. But here, Paul explained, our race centers around one goal: a life that's pleasing to God. And as any runner would tell you, it's much easier to persevere when you're fatigued than to quit and start all over again.

Father God, there are days I am weary. So, so weary that I don't take time to hear from You or I neglect my health. Or I get so ticked off at someone, I just explode. Or I indulge in retail therapy when I know I can't afford it. Lord, remind me that these seasons of weariness are episodes, not eternity. It's not forever. You are.

DISTRESS

You, who have shown me great and severe troubles,
Shall revive me again,
And bring me up again from the depths of the earth.

PSALM 71:20

ake a look around the beach. You probably see distressed wood, oxidized iron, and boats and dock posts fighting barnacles. In another time, these objects were new, pristine, pretty. But now they are chipped, dented, tired, careworn. They're no longer pretty, but their beauty remains. They wear the look of time, experience, hardships, and authenticity.

Maybe you're in a season where, like the distressed items, you feel past your prime. Perhaps you were pretty, or had a great career, or your children have moved out. You had this positive identity, but it no longer exists (sometimes by choice). Most days, you are at peace, but there are days when the "what-ifs" and "what-might-have-beens" creep in and, when they do creep in, guilt follows. As though we're not supposed to wonder or question the course of our lives.

Remember that distress in an everyday item usually occurs because the item is the best in its field. It has been useful and has the marks to prove it. Many a beach house or boat is furnished and decorated with distressed items; their display reminds us that what they did mattered for the long haul. Their contribution carried part of our world's story to the next step. The same holds true with people.

Extra pounds do not define your character. Fellow soccer moms don't know you used to be a CEO, but your children are blessed by your presence at their games. Your empty nest is an indication that you have helped provide the world with another generation of productive, responsible citizens. And you are by no means finished. Even though the sun has set on a particular point in your life, your work is not done.

The entirety of Psalm 71 is a remembrance of God's sovereignty over the life of the psalmist and the entire world. The writer saw himself as a "portent" to others— a sign or testimony of God's provision now and for the future, and he himself puts his trust in God, so that all he does may be to His glory. It's a good psalm to read when a door closes. It reminds us that, if we're still here, He is not finished. It's possible that your what-ifs will comingle with your what-nows . . . but even if you're taken in a completely different direction, trust that the closed chapter was purposeful and made an impact.

You see, your marks of distress are actually marks of distinction. Your life choices, your hurts, your victories—all are there on display. Your contribution carried our collective story to the next step. Your next contribution will too. And though we show blemishes and flaws—no longer to be defined as "pretty"—God restores us to great beauty.

Lord, let me ponder and meditate on the ways You have blessed my life. Let me also think of the many times You walked with me through fire and the lessons learned from each scar. Let my life stories serve as a testimony to Your glory—and together, let's move on to the next adventure.

BOULDER BEACHES

"The rain descended, the floods came, and the winds blew and beat on that house;
and it did not fall, for it was founded on the rock."

MATTHEW 7:25

If you've climbed on boulders like those found on beaches in the Pacific Northwest or New England, you've probably slipped a time or two. In many respects, we do the same thing in our commitment to Christ. But once you've ascended, once you're secure on this immovable structure and look out safely at the waves below, there is something truly remarkable in knowing that they may splash you, but they cannot carry you away.

There's a reason boulders are immune to storms: these large, sturdy rocks are anchored so deeply they are immovable. Some have been around for thousands of years, unmoved by time or conditions. They may be sat upon, rained upon, built around, or smoothed over, but the boulders remain intact.

In today's scripture, Jesus was talking about how to recognize His followers: they will be the ones who obey His teachings (v. 24), thereby building a secure foundation that will protect them.

Temptations and anguish have the same effect on our hearts that the waves have on us when we're seated on a boulder: they lap over us. At times, it may seem as though these waves are stronger than our rock, but as soon as they beat down on our foundation, they break and disperse.

Because of sin, we cannot avoid strife and difficulties on this side of heaven. But thanks to Christ, we have an eternal promise that He will break those hard times upon impact, giving us the power to manage and endure. "No temptation has overtaken you except such as is common to man; but God is faithful, who will not allow you to be tempted beyond what you are able, but with the temptation will also make the way of escape, that you may be able to bear it" (1 Corinthians 10:13).

Sit tight.

Lord, thank You for the visual of the boulder that endures rain, pests, waves, yet remains intact. Thank You that I am allowed to use Your teachings as my foundation, my rock, to use in the same manner when sin, temptations, and difficulties come my way.

SALT-AIR HAIR

There is no wisdom, no insight, no plan
that can succeed against the LORD.

PROVERBS 24:30 NIV

Why does our hair do that? You know, how it frizzes, frays, and frustrates as it flies around in the salty breeze.

You smooth it down. You may even comb conditioner through it. Or smooth it back with gel and wear it in a bun, pretending to go for that sleek, old-Hollywood effect. That'll work for a while, but eventually, you'll wash your hair. And dry it. And you don't even have to walk outside for the frizzies to reappear. Give it up! Salt-air hair is what it is.

Now today's verse, more than likely, wasn't written with salt-air hair in mind—but salt-air hair can remind us of this truth: there are just some things that are out of our control. And our best efforts, no matter how intelligent or skillful we are, cannot succeed against God.

We can laugh about this when it comes to frizzy beach hair. We can even try to embrace our not-quite curly locks—but there are times when it's not so funny. Times when by all accounts, evil seems to win: our child is being bullied, our best friend is making a wrong decision, we give into an addiction we think we've long ago conquered, our love has left us for another. And we want to retaliate or find another way to let them know that what they're doing is unacceptable—and maybe, just maybe, we'd like to hurt them back. Oh, we want to, and we play out the scenarios in our minds, because we can control how each scene unfolds.But real life doesn't work that way. And since God instructs us to let Him take care of these matters, our own schemes really won't work. In due time, either now or in the final tally, those who have wronged us will have to answer to God, as well. He is fair like that.

So celebrate this truth and leave the conditioner and hair gel behind today. Let your hair fly free as a reminder that your soul already does.

Father God, what a funny reminder of how little control I have—and how grateful I am for that. I don't have to worry about how to seek justice; You will take care of it one way or another. That frees me up on so many levels, and I praise You for this truth!

SOMETHING'S MISSING

Then Elkanah her husband said to her, "Hannah, why do you weep? Why do you not eat?
And why is your heart grieved? Am I not better to you than ten sons?"

1 SAMUEL 1:8

A boat without a sail . . . an empty net or nest . . . we can walk past these items a hundred times without glancing, but when a part of them is missing—particularly when we feel a part of us is missing something that "belongs"—we take notice.

Do you relate?

Hannah longed for a child. No other person could comfort her. Her well-intended husband discounted her feelings and questioned why he wasn't family enough for her. Perhaps your friends have lectured you about focusing on your blessings or are directing you to adoption Web sites.

Many times, although they are well intended, our loved ones reinforce additional feelings that something is "wrong" with us or that we are, somehow, inferior and that we don't see the picture as clearly. And it doesn't fix or change the desire. Our vulnerabilities are often better soothed by a tender hug and listening ear—and no commentary.

There is a difficult tension when the desires of your heart are out of reach, but they're commonplace for people around you, sometimes even taken for granted. And if God's promises hold true, where are the children that we long for? What about women like Sarah and Elizabeth? Where's our miracle? We live drama-free lives, have no known enemies, enjoy fulfilling careers, take care of ourselves, yet these longings remain unfulfilled.

If you're longing for a child, certainly emulate Hannah and continue to pray for God's direction. Maybe the timing isn't right yet, maybe He needs to give you peace about adoption, or maybe it's time to ask if your desires align with His. This is a scary step because it means letting go on such a deep and painful level. It may mean changing the focus of your time and energy, but it is the step that will ultimately yield peace, even a peace that surpasses our human understanding. Peter wrote, "For if these things are yours and abound, you will be neither barren nor unfruitful in the knowledge of our Lord Jesus Christ" (2 Peter 4:8).

In the meantime, you have many, many opportunities to express maternal feelings in ways that extend beyond motherhood. That part of you is *not* missing, so embrace it in a way God leads you.

Lord, You know my heart. I trust that there is more to my story, my longing for a child, that hasn't been revealed—and I pray fervently that Your revelation will come soon. Even more, I will trust Your timing. Give me peace and patience in the meantime and show me how my maternal instincts may be used to Your glory.

A SOUL AT REST

Return to your rest, O my soul,
For the LORD has dealt bountifully with you.
PSALM 116:7

What's your favorite way to relax at the beach? Nap in a hammock? Soak up rays? Enjoy the early morning breeze on a screened-in porch? Fish off the dock? Close your eyes and let the sound of the waves lull you away?

We are, by design, required to rest. Even Jesus needed sleep and downtime. It's an opportunity for our minds and bodies to replenish, relax, renew. Rest balances out our work and the stresses of everyday life.

But what does it mean for our *souls* to be at rest? What is the peace that Christ meant when He greeted His disciples after His resurrection (Luke 24:36)? Is it possible for our bodies and minds to be in motion and our souls to remain at rest? If so, how do we get there?

The author of Psalm 116 had not just been discouraged; he'd also experienced great suffering. He prayed, he cried—and he obeyed the command to be still, wait patiently, and not be afraid (Psalm 37:7). He was overcome with trouble and sorrow, but never once did he say he was afraid. He knew that times would be hard, yet he believed and was delivered. And he lived to express his joy over answered prayers and blessings . . . with his soul, once more, at rest.

As you rock in your hammock or have a quiet morning moment with coffee and your Bible, think about the times God has delivered you. Consider the blessings He has showered upon you. We cannot avoid strife and difficulties in this world, but these should not rattle your soul to unrest.

Father, how glorious it is relax in the calm of this place. The gentle, deep whispers of the waves, the distant bells on boats, and the breeze that embraces my face as though it's Your hand. Let me take a moment to simply enjoy the blessings and be grateful for the times that You have delivered me. I am reminded that, whether in the quiet or the calamity, my soul will be at rest because You are there. Like the psalmist, I believe.

BEACH HOUSES

*"You looked for much, but indeed it came to little;
and when you brought it home, I blew it away.
Why?" says the LORD of hosts.
"Because of My house that is in ruins,
while every one of you runs to his own house."*

HAGGAI 1:9

The beach houses of old, with all their charm and character, have given way to garish displays of excess. What once served as temporary housing for vacationers has become a game of Can-You-Top-This? for wealthy property owners. Valiant attempts to combat this, like the Crystal Cove Alliance, are fast becoming the exception instead of the rule.

Is this a by-product of a modern society's shift in values? Hardly. This kind of struggle existed long before the U.S. was founded, long before our Savior came into this world.

Haggai's is not a common go-to Bible story, but it is quite relevant to our world today. After their exile in Babylon, Jews returned to Jerusalem and were instructed to rebuild the temple. So they began . . . but somewhere along the way, as their self-interests soared, the temple work slowed.

Nothing satisfied them any longer. They had beautiful homes, plenty of food, and new clothes, but those were not the ways God *really* wanted to bless and prosper them. The prophet Haggai spoke to the people of their negligence, and next, he put the temple work in proper context. The temple work itself would not "save" anyone, but it would provide a place and, therefore, an opportunity to encourage holy living.

And holy living is the key to genuine satisfaction, not tending so much to their own self-interests.

Today, the correlation still doesn't make sense: what does tending to our churches and ministries have to do with us not liking anything in our closet? Or not liking our closets at all?

Just as the temple did, our minds, hearts, and spirits require rebuilding. Each day provides us another opportunity to rebuild and, over time, we become strong. New clothes, updated kitchens, and yes, even building a new beachfront home are all ways to celebrate God's provision, but they are not means to an end. These material items will not keep us strong or encourage us during difficulties, and they can be gone in an instant. This is why we are instructed to seek God's kingdom, His work, and His ways first (Matthew 6:33). Otherwise, we lose perspective.

Spoiler alert: Toward the end of the book of Haggai, the people laid the foundation for the temple again, and God blessed them at that moment (2:18–19). Did you catch that? God did not wait for the work to be completed before He blessed them. Their faithfulness in the first step—in that one, single step—brought forth blessings. So if He celebrates our first step, what awaits us at the point of completion?

Lord, I do get an unbalanced view of my possessions, and I can't always freely celebrate others' good fortunes. I do not want to insulate myself from Your work—I want to be a part of Your building process. And by doing so, I want You to be a part of my building process. Help me find Your perspective.

SUNRISES

So I have been allotted months of futility,
And wearisome nights have been appointed to me.
When I lie down, I say, "When shall I arise,
And the night be ended?"
For I have had my fill of tossing till dawn.

JOB 7:3-4

Tonight, even the waves do not soothe. You're restless.

Job was too. He had no idea why all of this was happening to him. He had done his best to be faithful. And he continued to do so. But he was at his wit's end.

Perhaps this is where you are tonight. Or maybe you're anxious about tomorrow. Or perhaps something else is gnawing at you, something from your past. If so, you're ensnared in something much more debilitating than just insomnia.

You need daylight to break through.

Sunrises hold so much promise: a new day, a new opportunity, a fresh start. If the night has failed you, get up and go watch the sun come up. Witnessing a sunrise at the beach is a soul-healing process. As the intense colors emerge from the horizon and break across the ocean, consider what our Lord said about worry: we are not to worry about tomorrow, for "sufficient for the day is its own trouble" (Matthew 6:34). And if past troubles are seeping into your todays, it's time to hand them over to the One who can erase them.

Whatever you said or did, you cannot go back and change. Nor can you predict the future. We cannot read minds or, like Job, always know exactly why bad things happen to us. Or why we don't have or can't see. We can move forward, crying out for God's sufficient grace each morning, knowing He will provide according to our need.

Dawn is coming. A fresh start. A new day. A clean slate.

Lord, thank You that, by Your Son, I receive grace and mercy. Thank You for the sunrise that reminds me that each day starts anew, and so can I. A brand-new day to start over, to Your glory.

OFF-PEAK SEASON

Though the LORD gives you
The bread of adversity and the water of affliction,
Yet your teachers will not be moved into a corner anymore,
But your eyes shall see your teachers.
Your ears shall hear a word behind you, saying,
"This is the way, walk in it,"
Whenever you turn to the right hand
Or whenever you turn to the left.

ISAIAH 30:20–24

A cold, lonely beach is a sad, mournful place. Choppy winds prohibit conversation and seem to blow in no particular direction. The sun provides little warmth; you bundle up and wander with its suggested emotion. Except for a rare day of good weather, off-peak season at any beach can be dreary and sad to those who expected something a little more inviting.

We have off-peak seasons in life too. Some experiences leave us devastated—things we had no control over, couldn't have predicted, and cannot explain nor justify. Events that simply happened to us. Situations that offer no closure.

And in fact, a lonely, cold beach can often be the appropriate setting to process some of our grief. We think through what our "new normal" will be, or we ask God to help us find a peace that does not require understanding.

These are not moments where we play victim because we truly *are* victims. We didn't do anything to cause what happened (though we will replay the events in our minds a million times, just to be sure). And any individuals involved will appear to have gotten away with their wrongdoing. Even if they're confronted and they repent, this would not remove the pain from your heart. It wouldn't be an even exchange. Where is God? And what are we expected to do now?

We grieve. We mourn. We also pray. We take our time, being careful to not miss a step in the process (and shortchange our own healing).

As the wind whips through your hair, think about how you are able to withstand the wind's taunts. As you stand or sit in silence, envision how strong He has made you, amid the calamity.

These are the times He chooses not to rescue us; these are the times He walks with us, saying, "This is the way, walk in it."

Lord, this may be a season that You do not carry me and You do not rescue me, but You do guide me in a definitive direction. I feel so alone. I do not understand, Father. I want to know why. I want to lash out, seek revenge, and wallow. That's what I want to do, but that's not what You have asked me to do. And ultimately I want to obey, so I will choose to trust. I may have to take this minute-by-minute, but I do trust You. And I will trust You. Forgive my stumbles, but do not let me miss a step in the way You want me to go.

GRAINS OF SAND

Then Judah said, "The strength of the laborers is failing,
and there is so much rubbish that we are not able to build the wall."

NEHEMIAH 4:10

Pick up a small handful of dry sand and really examine it. Look at the colors and how smoothly it passes through your fingers. Think about the tiny grains that together make up the entire beach. A small handful is easily moved, but moving an entire beach would be impossible.

Sometimes, there is strength in numbers; sometimes, *the numbers are given strength.*

Seventy years—that's how long the Israelites complained about the state of Jerusalem. It's so much easier, after all, to complain than to take action, work hard, and risk failure.

Thank goodness Nehemiah was not of the same opinion. Miraculously getting the proper permissions, Nehemiah organized the Israelites and began building. Confronted with ridicule and threats, the Israelites wilted. Debate, instead of work, ensued.

How many times have we gotten involved in a project, but never completed it? Or we begin a sentence with "Someday, I want to . . ." and then, the excuses rush in like a tidal wave. *We don't have enough help. We don't have enough money or time. No one else seems to think this is a good idea. Proceeding might lead to bigger problems.*

When God provided a way—and He did so in an unmistakable way—Nehemiah was given the responsibility of keeping projects organized and moving. He confronted those—both inside and outside the Israelite community—who tried to sabotage or give up on the work. He knew that God would not have brought His people this far to abandon them. Nehemiah knew that failure, in this case, would be due to disobedience.

So after complaining for seventy years, the Israelites managed to complete the city's wall in just fifty-two days. What an accomplishment!

Now as you pick up and examine another handful of sand, think again about how such tiny specks create such a large expanse. Watch how, individually, they blow in the wind, but when packed together they form a beach that may shift and change, yet always remains intact.

Is there something big you've written off as impossible? If God provides, are you willing to be responsible with what He's given you to do?

Lord, I think about those grains of sand and the Israelites who complained and debated, and their defeatist attitudes. If I'm tasked with a seemingly impossible project, I will trust You to provide the opportunities and to strengthen me. Give me an obedient heart, so that I will not be discouraged. And a grateful heart that I was chosen by You to organize and execute Your plans.

SAND FLEAS

And He said, "What comes out of a man, that defiles a man.
For from within, out of the heart of men,
proceed evil thoughts, adulteries, fornications, murders, thefts,
covetousness, wickedness, deceit, lewdness,
an evil eye, blasphemy, pride, foolishness.
All these evil things come from within and defile a man."

MARK 7:20-23

S and fleas are difficult to see, but you can feel their effects. And once they've gotten hold of you, it takes a professional to get rid of them.

Sand fleas really aren't fleas at all. They are crustaceans that swim, jump, and feed off the blood of humans and animals. If left unattended long enough, these tiny creatures can burrow under the skin, causing welts and illness.

They prefer pale skin since it's usually thinner and therefore easier to latch onto. They can penetrate anything within ten inches from the ground, so you'll typically find the bites around your ankles. Small dogs are especially subject to them, and an infestation requires the care of a physician or veterinarian.

Sin invades our lives in much the same way. At first, it's very small and subtle, beginning in our hearts and minds. Just entertaining sin a little here and there, we think we can handle it. When we pay enough attention, however . . . well, eventually, we can't pay it *enough* attention. It doesn't take long to get too big to remain in our minds—so then we act. That'll get rid of it once and for all, right? No? Maybe just one more time, then. Or maybe if we "trade" one action for another seemingly less harmful action . . .

Oh, we try any number of ways to escape the sin that has latched on. We even try to bargain with God.

Then we realize we're infested.

We all face temptation and tests. Whether either leads to sin is up to us. Whether in our speech or deeds, once sin grabs hold, it's very difficult for it not to travel outwardly into our actions. And not only do we hurt ourselves, we also hurt others.

Just like a sand-flea infestation—we require the care of the Great Physician.

Lord, I need You as my Helper when it comes to self-control. Show me a better way than what I find myself tempted to do. Remind me that joy and communion with You are so much better than anything the world or the Enemy offers.

SALT WATER

My brothers and sisters, can a fig tree bear olives, or a grapevine bear figs?
Neither can a salt spring produce fresh water.

JAMES 3:12 NIV 2011

Do you remember the first time you tasted the salt water of the ocean? Were you gently warned? If so, did you really believe the warning to be true? If not, was it a shock to your system? If so, was the salty taste *still* a shock to your system?

Anger—our own or someone else's—can be a shock to the system too. We try to catch our breath, but we're so inflamed with hurt or pride that the breath won't come. Just like the first time we discovered the ocean's salty water, we're startled in a way that leaves us breathless.

Does your speech or behavior affect others the same way? Do you take into account how you deliver your words or how you act in certain situations? Are your words and actions "with grace, *seasoned* with salt" (Colossians 4:6, emphasis added), or are they a shock to your system and to the one on the receiving end?

The tongue is a tricky mechanism. It can build up or level a person swifter than anything. James referred to it as "unruly evil, full of deadly poison" (v. 3:8). When our speech or delivery contradicts how Jesus taught us to be, it confuses people around us. The same holds true of our behavior. Deeds that contradict Jesus' commands indicate a gap between who we are and who we claim to be.

So when is showing anger justified? How do we reprimand or confront others without "losing it"? How do we make a point without being abrasive or hurtful?

First of all, figure out *why* you're angry—especially if it's preventing you from seeing any wrongdoing on your part. Honestly whittle down to the real reason for it. Second, if discipline or confrontation must ensue, get a grip on yourself before proceeding. Remember, the goal is to reconcile, not retaliate. And do not let your anger fester. A timely response is more prudent than waiting and letting your anger build past the boiling point. Ask God for help with each of these steps. Ask Him to provide the right words and the ability to speak the truth in love (Ephesians 4:15). Finally, prepare yourself for a possibly adverse response or denial. Decide beforehand that you will respond with great caution, keeping peaceful resolve at the forefront of your mind.

If you owe someone an apology, then do it. Be sincere and ask for forgiveness. Regardless of whether you're on the giving or receiving end of an apology—or whether you should receive one, but don't—accept that sometimes forgiveness is not conditional nor instantaneous. But with God's help, it will come. That too is a measure of who we are versus who we claim to be.

Lord, as I splash about in the salt water today, remind me of the effects of my speech and behavior. Help me search and rid my heart of any grudges or hurts that remain, replacing them with a seed of forgiveness You will grow. If I need to confront or apologize to someone, help me come to terms with this and move forward. As Your child, I want to be who I claim to be.

WIPEOUT

Finally, all of you be of one mind, having compassion for one another; love as brothers, be tenderhearted, be courteous; not returning evil for evil or reviling for reviling, but on the contrary blessing, knowing that you were called to this, that you may inherit a blessing.

1 PETER 3:8–9

There you are, minding your own business, relaxing in your beach chair with a magazine. Or you've hit that lull between awake and sleep, where you still hear the sounds around you, but they seem rather distant.

Then, *WHAM!* You're jarred awake by a wave that crashes right over you, taking away your cooler of goodies, sunglasses, and cell phone. You jump to your feet, and there goes your chair and towel. You scramble to pick up what you can before the tide carries it away, and *WHAM!* another wave hits! Your arms are full, and you don't have time to run your things up to the dunes. On and on, the waves lap over you, determined to retrieve all of your relaxation accoutrements. You stand on the shore, shocked and defeated, as all calmly drifts away and sinks.

We can be overtaken in life too. Not overwhelmed, but *overtaken.* Your husband gave in to the flirtations of his coworker and now wants a divorce. Your five-year-old has just been diagnosed with leukemia, *and* you don't have medical insurance. The bank has just foreclosed on your home, and your family has nowhere to go but a homeless shelter.

Regardless of what overtakes us, our dreams are shattered and we're numb. Well-intentioned friends keep telling us about the "new normal" we have to find, but we're just trying to survive the day, the hour, the minute. Our world stopped, yet everyone else's keeps on turning.

Look back at Peter's words. *Compassion. Tenderhearted. Blessing.* And the tough phrase—*called to this.* Not *called* like those who are called to preach, use a talent, or start a ministry—but *called* in the sense that you have arrived at this place of despair, overtaken by something that was out of your control.

But not out of the Almighty God's.

There is blessing to be found in our darkest moments. It may be something simple, like your child eating food and keeping it down. It may be something huge, like an anonymous donor paying your mortgage. Or it may be something unknown for many, many years. Ask God to keep you tenderhearted so that you spot His blessings, large or small. Commit to treating others with compassion and respect, even if they do not treat you that way. And remind yourself that He has clothed you with strength and dignity (Proverbs 31:25) to not only survive, but to live life abundantly.

Lord, I felt utterly powerless after _____ happened. Some days I need strength just to hold my head up. Remind me that I am valuable to You. Keep my heart tender in spite of any attacks. Reveal, in Your timing, the blessing in all this—because, Father, I do not see it. I cannot find it. I need Your eyes, Your ears, Your heart.

SURFING GOOD WAVES

Fear not, for I have redeemed you;
I have called you by your name;
You are Mine.
When you pass through the waters, I will be with you;
And through the rivers, they shall not overflow you.

ISAIAH 43:1–2

There is something otherwordly about a surfer who rides inside a wave. Granted, those who ride the crest seem to defy gravity, but the surfers who dare to climb inside are not attempting to conquer it. They remain inside, directing the choreography of the ride, because the wave is the vehicle that carries them. They've managed to paddle, stand, balance, and climb inside, but the surfers have to discern quickly how they're going to orchestrate the journey successfully. And as any surfer will tell you, their decisions aren't always right.

We have days when everything happens at once. Yes, even good things. And even though we hear ourselves saying, "These are good problems to have," we start to get that overwhelmed feeling, and then we may feel guilty or unappreciative. Multiple job offers after months of desperately searching; two different children receiving awards on the same day, at the same time; many social invitations for the same date; leadership nominations; or any combination of such things—these *are* good problems to have, because they likely indicate that we are in demand, have achieved a goal, or have shown noticeable integrity. So let's not discount how wonderful that is!

Unfortunately, sometimes we drown in the "overwhelmingness" of doing it all instead of taking even a nanosecond to step back and be present with God.

Sometimes He will equip us supernaturally with divine stamina and wisdom. Other times, He may help us see that we have choices to make and will instill in us the power to say no.

So when we do take time to be present and acknowledge His presence with us, His gentle guidance helps us paddle, stand, balance, and finally, climb inside. With the assurance of His help, we can be grateful and amazed at the outpouring of blessing instead of being washed away by its current.

Father, thank You so much for the wonderful blessings that You put in my life. I am overwhelmed with joy, not stress. I ask for wisdom to help me navigate; for strength and clear-headedness to be present; and for willingness to say no at Your direction, no matter how much coercion or how strong the tactics others may use.

THE L WORD

You shall love the L<small>ORD</small> your God with all your heart,

with all your soul, and with all your strength.

D<small>EUTERONOMY</small> 6:5

The beach simply lends itself to romance—to long walks along the surf, casual dinners overlooking a harbor, relaxing on the sand, evening boat tours. It can be the perfect setting for couples to relax and just enjoy each other's company, whether they are reigniting their love or discovering it for the first time.

The beach is also a perfect setting to reignite our love for God—or for some, to discover it for the first time.

How often do we say, "I love You" to the Lord? We know we love Him. We know He loves us. But how often do we *say* it with full and grateful hearts? As we're absorbing His creation, at the beach or even in our own homes, do we take a moment to snap a mental picture and remember to let Him know how much we love Him? Is it possible that *saying* it may be another way to love Him with "all our strength"?

God pursues us. He listens. He understands. He reassures us. He keeps His promises. He provides. He gives good gifts. If any human being were to do this much for us, we'd most certainly let that person know.

So why not say "thank You" to the One who breathed us into existence?

Lord, I love You. I simply don't tell You enough or how much. I am so thankful You are in my life, thankful for Your many, many blessings, and even thankful for the trials, for I know they ultimately bring us closer. I love You.

SHELTER

You have been a refuge for the poor,
a refuge for the needy in his distress,
a shelter from the storm
and a shade from the heat.
For the breath of the ruthless
is like a storm driving against a wall.

Isaiah 25:4 NIV

B each storms can arrive quickly, sometimes with devastating consequences. If you've ever been caught in one, particularly on a boat, the rain can feel like needles on your skin. Lightning can be deadly. Whether you make it back to your rental house, your car, or even just a covered structure, finding shelter is a priority—your only priority. Once you're covered, you feel safe. Once inside, you are relieved.

Storms pop up in everyday life too. We can't predict their arrivals or departures. So, what does it mean to find refuge in God? What does it mean to find shelter from the heat and the pressures of our earthly lives? Where do we find the practical in such a seemingly ethereal concept?

While it's true that this verse deals specifically with physical poverty, the passage goes on to describe how those who wait patiently on God will be delivered—a prophecy of what's to come.

In terms of practicality, the "shelter" God provides may come in the form of another person's help—a job lead, a contrite heart, an apology. However it arrives, trust that if He's provided it, relief will follow. We need only step out in faith, honoring and obeying through our actions. But there is a Part II.

Let's not just think in terms of physical poverty. Consider *spiritual* poverty, as well. In the Old Testament times, spiritual issues were often addressed before physical relief arrived; God wanted repentance before restoration. This hasn't changed. But if you think about it, Jesus often met the physical needs of others *before* He ever addressed the spiritual. Jesus did not heal the sick, drive out demons, or feed the masses—all very practical, physical needs—without pointing to God and the Way to true peace that's everlasting. Jesus did this so that, even today as we seek shelter and refuge, believers fulfill what was stated in Isaiah 25:9: "And it will be said in that day: 'Behold, this is our God; we have waited for Him, and He will save us. This is the Lord; we have waited for Him; we will be glad and rejoice in His salvation.'"

It's very practical and very wise to seek refuge from storms and relief from God in all of life's storms—but don't expect Him to meet your physical needs without addressing the spiritual, as well. You will be changed, inside and out.

Lord, today I am reminded of the way You delivered me during _____. From that, I learned that there remained a part of me I had not entrusted to You. Search my heart and unlock any doors that remain shut so that I may know and declare Your provision. I will wait, and I will take refuge in You. Please use this current storm to draw me closer to You.

WAVE JUMPING

Where were you when I laid the earth's foundations?
Tell me, if you understand. . . .
Who shut up the sea behind doors
when it burst forth from the womb. . . .
when I said, 'This far you may come and no farther;
here is where your proud waves halt'?"

JOB 38:4, 8, 11 NIV

We run toward the waves until we are a few feet in. Then, turning so our backs face the ocean, we scream, hold our breath, and jump each time a wave hits us. Why? We've done this hundreds of times. We're not so far out that we'll be carried away. We know what it feels like and what to expect, yet we do it every time.

Perhaps there's a small part of us that doesn't really believe we'll have the same outcome. Maybe, just maybe, the next wave will be the one—the giant wave that, instead of lifting us up, rises above the others and claps twenty feet down on top of us, and carries us away to a faraway place.

When it comes to jumping waves, we *know* how it's done . . . but we don't necessarily *believe* it will work every time. In the same way, we can hesitate because of unbelief in our prayer lives.

God has become more of a cultural fixture than our living, eternal Creator. Many times, we *know* God—He's there, He's in charge—but we still don't *believe* Him. There are pockets of ourselves we're unwilling to hand over. We fear He will reject us once and for all, or that part of us will be something He can't handle.

While we proudly display our "God Bless America" signs and decorative crosses, pray Elizabethan-esque prayers, or rhetorically credit Him for our latest success, we can't seem to give Him five minutes out of our busy days. We know there's a God, but we don't *get to know* Him. We believe there's a God, but we don't *believe in* Him. He's up there in the clouds, disconnected from our day-to-day lives. Besides, He might not be there to catch us when the next wave crashes. We shouldn't count on it. At least, that's what our flesh tells us.

At the next opportunity, try standing with your back toward the ocean. Don't look for the next wave. Keep breathing, and remain silent as the wave crashes into your back and grabs your ankles. Remain steady as the undertow seems to be taking you down. It's going to feel unnatural at first, because it goes against your reflexes. Now, think about your private communions with God. Do you wait for a crashing wave to send you screaming toward Him? Or do you keep breathing and stay silent, knowing you will hear His voice, no matter what hits you?

Lord, I confess that sometimes I wait until a crisis hits, yet then it feels unnatural to pray, like I'm asking a stranger for a favor. So please! Reach deep inside my heart and mind, Lord, and scrub my doubt away. Let me know, in a way that might not make sense to anyone else, that You are there and that You are the great I Am.

SEASHELLS

For the poor will never cease from the land; therefore I command you, saying,
"You shall open your hand wide to your brother,
to your poor and your needy, in your land."

DEUTERONOMY 15:11

Seashells come in all shapes and sizes. There are so many varieties—conch, scallop, clam, oyster, cowry—and then there are varieties within the varieties. The selections and quantities certainly differ at high and low tides and even more so after a storm. Our collections may last a day, or a lifetime. But what about the broken ones? Do we ever stop for them?

We can ask the same about the people we encounter any given day. Just like seashells, we certainly have our favorites—the ones we seek out, ones we notice. Others we discover by accident or circumstance, and we're grateful to have them too. Some encounters result in lifelong relationships, while others may last only a few minutes.

But what about the broken people? Do we see them? Really, really see them?

Sometimes they are very obviously broken, and we look away as we walk past, unable to bear their presence, wishing they'd just make themselves whole again. They are easy to ignore and overlook. On others, the fractures are barely visible until we're too close to their situations. As much as we'd like to look away or act as though we don't see, it's too late. And we feel stuck with their fragments until we can think of some excuse to put some distance between us. We can't have drama. We do not want to risk exposure to someone's instability or hardship, lest it burden us.

But "you shall open your hand wide to your brother."

We are to care for and meet the needs of the broken as though we are caring for the Lord Himself. Because—and He's very clear about this—He instructs us to (Matthew 25:40). It is as though we're caring for Him.

It also bears mentioning that "poor" and "needy" can apply to the fiscal, physical, mental, and spiritual conditions of a person. So tomorrow, it could be you.

Pick up a shell fragment and carry it for a while as a reminder that, just like seashells, no two people are the same. Some are whole. Some are broken. All are beautiful.

Dear Lord, help me notice those who are broken and not shy away from those whose cracks emerge upon closer inspection or emerge at a later time. As I care for them, I am reminded this could be me—or this could be You.